40p

STUDIES IN ENGLISH LITERATURE

*General Editor*

David Daiches
Dean of the School of English and American Studies,
University of Sussex

To
EITHNE

# SHAKESPEARE: MUCH ADO ABOUT NOTHING

by
## J. R. MULRYNE

*Lecturer in English Literature, The University, Edinburgh*

EDWARD ARNOLD

© J. R. MULRYNE 1965

*First published 1965 by*
Edward Arnold (Publishers) Ltd.,
41 Maddox Street, London, W.1

*Reprinted 1969*

Boards edition SBN: 7131 5082 3
Paper edition SBN: 7131 5083 1

*Printed in Great Britain by*
*The Camelot Press Ltd., London and Southampton*

# General Preface

It has become increasingly clear in recent years that what both the advanced sixth former and the university student need most by way of help in their literary studies are close critical analyses and evaluations of individual works. Generalisations about periods or authors, general chat about the Augustan Age or the Romantic Movement, have their uses; but all too often they provide merely the illusion of knowledge and understanding of literature. All too often students come up to the university under the impression that what is required of them in their English literature courses is the referring of particular works to the appropriate generalisations about the writer or his period. Without taking up the anti-historical position of some of the American 'New Critics', we can nevertheless recognise the need for critical studies that concentrate on the work of literary art rather than on its historical background or cultural environment.

The present series is therefore designed to provide studies of individual plays, novels and groups of poems and essays, which are known to be widely studied in sixth forms and in universities. The emphasis is on clarification and evaluation; biographical and historical facts, while they may of course be referred to as helpful to an understanding of particular elements in a writer's work, will be subordinated to critical discussion. What kind of work is this? What exactly goes on here? How good is this work, and why? These are the questions which each writer will try to answer.

DAVID DAICHES

# Acknowledgements

Quotations from *Much Ado* are taken from the Signet Classic edition, edited by David L. Stevenson. I have found this the most convenient and helpful edition for student use. Quotations from other Shakespeare plays are taken from the Oxford three-volume text.

Some acknowledgement of indebtedness to earlier critics is made in the essay itself; the list of recommended reading includes other books and essays I have found helpful. A more general debt is owed to friends and students at Edinburgh, Birmingham and Cambridge.

# Contents

# 1. Introductory

An adequate reading of one of Shakespeare's 'mature comedies' presents certain difficulties; many a reader closes his text puzzled and disappointed. But such a reaction is very much less usual in the theatre; it is commonplace that these plays produce, given the bare necessities, very satisfyingly. A sense of exuberant and uninhibited vitality, of an irrepressibly rich invention, of an outlook that critics like to call, in despair of a more precisely defining term, 'life-enhancing' comes across very vividly. We go from the theatre with an imaginative knowledge of the abundance of life, a belief (provisional certainly) in its essential goodness. And yet when we look at the text we may find ourselves wondering where all the vitality has drained to; we may even begin to make radical criticisms of the play itself, criticisms of a kind that failed to exercise our minds in the theatre. Quite obviously we must learn to read in a manner sensitive to the potential (and the limitations) of stage production if we are to take in the riches the play has to offer; and we must neither be disappointed nor carp if we fail to discover satisfactions of a different order. Reading a play is, or should be, an activity quite distinct from reading a poem or novel.

This point must be made at the outset, since *Much Ado* is commonly held to be 'deeply flawed' because it fails to satisfy certain criteria of probability which a desk-bound critic—and critics are simply articulate readers—finds himself imposing. Such adverse criticism centres round the nominal main-plot, the Hero/Claudio liaison, and focuses especially on the personality and behaviour of Claudio himself. We shall have more to say about this later, but for the moment taking issue with one of the more frequently-repeated assertions—that Claudio's remorse at the death of Hero is totally unconvincing— will serve to emphasise the need for a theatre-conscious reading of the text.

Shakespeare chooses to render this remorse chiefly in Act V, scene iii, a mere thirty lines or so of verse, including six lines of rhymed epitaph and ten lines of song. To a visually unreceptive reading it makes very little impression; the mere reading of one rather undistinguished verse and the singing of another, followed by a resolve to repeat the practice yearly. But if the reader can respond imaginatively to the possibilities of theatre, these slight indications grow into impressively meaningful experience. We must try to visualise the setting. On the modern stage, the atmosphere will be gloomy, a dull backdrop and low lighting; the costumes (on any stage) will be dark, perhaps of black; a slow procession carrying flickering torches will encircle the stage, perhaps chanting, and group before some property representing 'Hero's tomb'. Shakespeare is careful to conjure up forcefully (crudely even) the appropriate associations

> Midnight, assist our moan;
> Help us to sigh and groan,
> Heavily, heavily.
> Graves, yawn and yield your dead,
> Till death be utterèd,
> Heavily, heavily. (V. iii. 16-21)

The effect, in the theatre, is totally dispiriting; a dead, slack, apparently sterile calm. And what takes merely seconds to read, is several minutes in performance. The audience undergoes, in fact, an experience that is deeply impressive at the time and distinctly memorable during the rest of the play and when it is over. An ill-defined experience certainly, not one that investigates Claudio's remorseful consciousness, or specifies his moral reflection on his behaviour. But this is precisely what Shakespeare wants at this point. With the play developing as it has, moral analysis would be entirely out of place; to interest us now in the idiosyncratic movements of Claudio's mind would open up perspectives the play has not otherwise explored. We need only be assured about the depth of Claudio's emotional response, not its precise nature: and this the theatrical experience to which the words-on-the-page appropriately give rise will do for us. To describe Claudio's remorse as too slight to be convincing (and therefore too slight to regain our sympathy for him) is to misread the play, to read it as one would properly read a novel, without allowance for the visual (and of course aural) realisation that performance achieves.

The visualising imagination essential to a balanced estimate of the 'tomb' scene enables the reader to respond fully to other scenes also. The masked ball (II. i.), for example, must be acted in the mind's eye if we are to appreciate the brilliant deftness of the humour, its patterned ironies, and, more especially, if we are to take in to the full the importance of this scene for the play's thematic investigation of illusion. Something of this will come across, certainly, to a visually-unreceptive reading; but a mere spectre only of the full imaginative impact that comes with visual awareness: the brilliantly-dressed figures moving in the conventional (and complicated) measures of the dance, each behind the impassive, assumed countenance of the mask hiding a face that registers the speaker's real emotions—and these often contrary to the overt meaning of his words. Only a three-dimensional image of this kind can do justice to Shakespeare's comic invention. The same is true also of the twin scenes in which Benedick and then Beatrice are duped into a 'mountain of affection' for each other. The actual presence of the victim, reacting with gesture and facial expression to the overheard conversation, very notably enriches the humour of the scenes; as does the assumed demeanour of the tricksters—a grave countenance, bearing and tone of voice punctuated by nods and winks and natural-voiced asides. So one could go on to demonstrate how every scene is enriched by visualisation: the comic repartee between Benedick and Beatrice, often so apparently wire-drawn on the page, becomes warmly humorous as each reacts to the other's slanders. And Dogberry and Verges, marvellously comic as their dialogue undeniably is, become even more richly absurd as their pretensions are measured against their physical reality and that of their fellows. Visual imagination is, in short, an essential adjunct to an adequate and balanced reading of *Much Ado*.

We may pause for a moment to ask why, apart from the immediate advantages just outlined, an insistence upon visual awareness is so essential when discussing the comedies. What is it that sets them apart from Shakespeare's other dramatic work, and perhaps goes some way towards explaining the dearth of really convincing critical writing about them? A reading of any of Shakespeare's plays is enhanced by visual imagination; they were, after all, created with performance in mind. But with the tragedies in particular, the essential experience of the play inheres so substantially in language, is so richly communicated by imagery and metaphor (as well as, of course, by the development of event) that a non-visualised reading gives access to the play's central 'meaning'. (Visualisation as we are using the term is quite distinct from the visualisation inseparable from understanding metaphor.) Whereas the comedies at every point imply the three dimensions of performance: language without question still (as we shall see) matters; but activity matters importantly too. The comic experience is as much that of a world in motion as of a world verbalised. And while the tragedies focus characteristically upon the interior consciousness of an individual (and invoke the external world largely as mirror of, or comment on, that consciousness) the comedies are most notably occupied with *relationships*, with the interaction of a number of briefly-created personalities. We think of how Olivia and Orsino, Viola and Sebastian, Sir Toby, Maria and Sir Andrew combine (or interact rather) to form the comic world of *Twelfth Night*; of how Rosalind and Orlando, Touchstone and Audrey, Silvius and Phoebe—and Jacques—act like angled mirrors to reflect and distort each other's ideals in *As You Like It*; of how court, fairies and mechanicals are drawn together in *A Midsummer Night's Dream* in a series of mutually illuminating encounters. This is how these plays work, in contrast to the simpler development of the tragedies (even allowing for sub-plot development in *Lear*); to respond to them we have to build their meaning out of a series of related facets, and not, as normally with the tragedies, to explore in ever-increasing richness a situation present in germ from the beginning. So that stage performance, or the visualising we can substitute in reading, is essential to place those facets substantially before us, to enable us to appreciate fully the contrasting interests that spell meaning in these plays, and, sometimes, to allow us to see the activities that rehearse in miniature essential concerns. And in addition to take in the diverse meanings of action the disciplined kaleidoscope of theatre provides. In this inheres the vitality of theatre production so often lacking in desk-bound reading; and impossible for the critic fully to transmit when he writes of these plays—his words cannot mimic the rich three-dimensional simultaneity of stage-production.

This raises at once the whole question of critical competence, of what we can properly hope to do in the following pages. It might seem a logical deduction from what we have just been saying that the critic is impertinent to attempt to deal with a Shakespeare comedy, since he cannot, by admission, convey the vitality of theatre-production, nor even of its shadow, a visually-aware reading. And yet to deny the critic the right to discuss the play as a literary text is to overlook one undeniable fact: the only stable term in the whole business of theatre is the text, the words-on-the-page. With Shakespeare in particular, apart from a few shadowy and rather uncertain stage-directions, the text is the single clue we have as to how the author imagined his play. Every valid production can only, therefore, be rooted in a sensitive reading of the text, a reading that attempts by unprejudiced scrutiny to discover the governing themes and concerns that give the play as a *literary* achievement its integrity. The producer (if he is to give us more than a gimmicky, wilful distortion) must develop from here his fully-realised production, allowing the discovered themes to fertilise every speech and every scene he works on. He will naturally recognise as he reads theatrical opportunities, imagine bits of 'business' that will take and hold an audience's attention; but he must develop them only if they accord with the initial discoveries he makes as he reads the text. And it is with these initial discoveries that the critic is properly concerned. We shall remain alert, as we have been saying, to the visual activity implied immediately by the text, and we shall be conscious that we cannot recreate in words the vital experience of theatre; with that assistance and that admission we can properly begin to discover the essential concerns of *Much Ado*.

## 2. The Large Design

If we were challenged to state, in general terms, the 'subject' of Shakespeare's early and mature comedies, we could properly reply 'love'. Or more precisely, 'love in courtship'. Their plots centre round the initial or consequent difficulties that stand in the way of love, and end with love's eventual triumph in marriage. They share the assumption that true intersexual love represents the highest good (male friendship, so highly valued by the Elizabethans, is barely dealt with) and make such love at once the standard of moral judgement and the subject of a delighted exploratory study. Each of the five most rewarding comedies —*The Merchant of Venice, A Midsummer Night's Dream, Much Ado, As You Like It, Twelfth Night*—concerns itself importantly with the nature of a lover's experience: its social and personal implications, its strength and its precariousness, its delusions, contradictions, exaltations and humiliations, and (before the debasement of the word) its enchantments. When we attempt for the first time, therefore, to explore the essential meaning of *Much Ado*, it will be useful to consider the fortunes of love-in-courtship as primary guide.

The overall design of *Much Ado* is not difficult to grasp. Basically the play is composed of three movements, the first (and longest) establishing the love-relationship between Benedick and Beatrice and between Claudio and Hero; the second portraying a crisis (when Don John's treachery causes the repudiation of Hero and her 'death'); and the third providing a resolution, as the deceit is exposed and a 'new' Hero marries a remorseful Claudio, and Beatrice Benedick. The comic thesis of the play in other words takes the form of love begun, love challenged and love confirmed: we are first made sympathetically aware of the love of two young couples (one pair willingly acknowledging love's claims, the other reluctantly); next, a malicious intrigue threatens to wreck all thoughts of joy and love; and finally life sails out into the clear once more, with a new strength and promise of endurance.

Each of Shakespeare's mature comedies holds in some measure a threat to the happiness of the figures for whom our sympathy is invited; in *Much Ado* our sense of comic triumph, of 'pleasurable reassurance' that 'all shall be well', is strong in proportion to the prominence given to the possibility of disaster. Only *The Merchant of Venice* gives equal weight to the threat that faces the protagonists. And so, when the play ends in double marriage (or rather in the dance that symbolises the concord of marriage) we enjoy vicariously a sense of good now established all the more firmly and valuably by virtue of the testing adversity to which it has been subjected. Characteristically, Shakespeare has anticipated the nature of this experience by figuring it in miniature in the first few lines of the play:

*Messenger.* . . . He [Claudio] hath borne himself beyond the promise of his age, doing, in the figure of a lamb, the feats of a lion. He hath indeed better bett'red expectation than you must expect of me to tell you how.

*Leonato.* He hath an uncle here in Messina will be very much glad of it.

*Messenger.* I have already delivered him letters, and there appears much joy in him; even so much that joy could not show itself modest enough without a badge of bitterness.

*Leonato.* Did he break out into tears?

*Messenger.* In great measure.

*Leonato.* A kind overflow of kindness. There are no faces truer than those that are so washed. How much better is it to weep at joy than to joy at weeping! (I. i. 13-28)

It is an experience of this nature, joy tempered by (modified and rendered more valid by) 'weeping' that the play will offer us.

To speak in these terms, while a useful guide to the basic 'shape' of the play, is very far from precise enough. We must take the feel of the various episodes much more carefully if we are to appreciate, even on this initial, very general, level, the individual experience offered by *Much Ado*. Critics have never been in doubt as to the dominant figures of the play's first movement; some of the earliest references to *Much Ado* actually name the play 'Beatrice and Benedick'. Nor is there dispute about the type of experience these two figures convey. 'The mirth of Beatrice (and no less that of Benedick) is an outbreak of the joyous energy of life' (Dowden); '. . . the exuberant quality of lively minds which strike fire by scoring off each other . . . *competitive* vitality' (Rossiter); 'gay, light-hearted critics of every illusion' (J. R. Brown). These are phrases typical of the agreed response: abundant vitality, gaiety, self-confidence, a brilliantly witty command of language, are the qualities all of us respond to, and which bulk large in our experience of the play's initial movement. We have our first taste of their 'competitive vitality' very early. Shakespeare allows the messenger and Leonato to make the thematic point about joy and weeping, and then a distinctive voice cuts across the rather formal, even awkward and halting exchange —a capable actress can make much of this opportunity—to pose a question in a quite different idiom:

*Beatrice.* I pray you, is Signior Mountanto returned from the wars or no?

The voice is distinctive partly because, as Hero immediately explains, it is unwilling to espouse even the most ordinary conventions; the irrepressible mockery that burgeons as the scene goes on here refuses to Benedick even the courtesy of his own name. And a few moments later there is another voice in concert with this one, each vying with the other to weave the more fanciful, witty and outrageous tracery of words. endlessly inventive and endlessly reckless of convention and simple truth. The first set of wit they play is typical of many to follow:

*Benedick.* What, my dear Lady Disdain! Are you yet living?
*Beatrice.* Is it possible Disdain should die while she hath such meet food to feed it as Signior Benedick? Courtesy itself must convert to Disdain if you come in her presence.
*Benedick.* Then is courtesy a turncoat. But it is certain I am loved of all ladies, only you excepted; and I would I could find in my heart that I had not a hard heart; for truly I love none. (I. i. 114-23)

And so on, almost inexhaustibly. We take delight in their carefree self-reliance, their refusal to acknowledge any claims but those of their own wit. Even as we recognise that they are engaged (whether conscious of it or not) in a common form of preliminary flirtation. And when their friends ease them, in parallel scenes rich in opportunities for comic by-play (as we have noted), into a hesitant recognition of their mutual affection, the play's dominant mood does not alter. Our experience is still one very largely of non-responsible gaiety. So all-pervasive, indeed, is this mood, that when we look back on the first movement, we scarcely remember the bethrothal of Claudio and Hero, nor Don John's sideline villainy. These characters and their affairs seem no more than necessary episodes in a plot whose main purpose is to give life to Beatrice and

Benedick, and the emotional and intellectual experience they convey. And this, on an overall view, is to see them in proper perspective. For the moment, gaiety and non-responsibility dominate. In later pages we shall have much more to say about other aspects of the first movement, and about a fully critical response to Beatrice and Benedick, but nothing is to be gained by expanding on these now; the salient features are clear.

The point of turn comes in Act III scene ii. As Benedick exits with Leonato to 'break' about his love for Beatrice (that situation, we think, is happily concluded; now 'the two bears will not bite one another when they meet'), Don John enters to initiate his malicious plot against Hero—an instance this of the fine dovetailing of event that characterises the whole *Much Ado* narrative. We move at once from a world of carefree gaiety, where the characteristic activity of language was a free and zestful elaboration, into a world that is cold and purposeful, a world of economic, even staccato utterance. Don John's careful qualification of 'disloyal' exemplifies the new temper:

*Don John.* The word is too good to paint out her wickedness. I could say she were worse. Think you of a worse title, and I will fit her to it. Wonder not till further warrant. (III. ii. 105-8)

Where a single word had been, on Beatrice's lips or Benedick's, the impetus to an exuberant, fertile inventiveness, it is now the occasion for meticulous adjustment; language has grown unfruitful, open only to grudging dissection. Don John's accusation of Hero shows the same withholding brevity:

*Don John.* I came hither to tell you, and, circumstances short'ned (for she has been too long a-talking of), the lady is disloyal. (III. ii. 98-100)

An audience or reader cannot but respond to this altogether different emotional climate; the exhilaration of a few moments ago modulates into a sense of cold malice, a malice far more formidable than Don John had hitherto seemed to represent. In a moment the entire positive and reassuring drive of the play towards marriage has been halted, and we are plunged into a world where the obstacles to successful courtship may be substantial. We must allow ourselves to visualise a new gravity on the face of Claudio and Don Pedro, a new and colder tone in their voices, a new stiffness in their posture and movements. Sensitive production could convey the new temper very forcefully.

B

Shakespeare exercises a nice control over the extent of an audience's or a reader's involvement in this threatening new world; the next scene introduces for the first time Dogberry, Verges and the Watch, figures of sufficient humorous weight to counterbalance the villainies of Don John and his henchmen. We enter unaffectedly into the world of official bumbledom to which Dogberry introduces us; we delight in his self-importance, his garrulous inconsequence, his huge and magnificent absurdity. And yet the Dogberry world merely *balances* that of Don John, it does not cancel it; it relieves tension sufficiently to preserve the comic hypothesis of 'all shall be well'—the mould would crack otherwise—but without in any way preventing us from responding with appropriate gravity to the other and contrary scenes in this movement. We shall have more to say about Dogberry later; for the moment it is best to concentrate on the graver aspects in this section of the play.

It is in this connection that comment on the play, whether in print or verbal, often seems least adequate. Critics, unanimous and vocal in discussing Beatrice and Benedick, are equally unanimous and vocal in their treatment of the Watch. But lengthy and appreciative discussion of the 'Church' scene (IV. i.) and of some other, grave, episodes at this point in the play, is indeed rare. Despite this, an appeal to any serious remembered performance, or to a sensitive, visually-receptive reading, will confirm that these dark scenes bulk large in our experience; it is only through the distortion that non-imagining reading gives that they appear inconsiderable. Let us see what a critically alert, visually-conscious reading will make of at least the more obvious features of these episodes.

It is worth noticing, to begin with, that they are consciously and overtly 'theatrical': the setting and the properties suggested, as well as the language, help to press our experience right up to the frontiers of melodrama. In the 'Church' scene itself, we must see with the mind's eye the lighted candles and the monk's garb, the altar and the other church-like 'props', and take in the sense of formal decorum the group-ing and gestures would imply. This is a solemn occasion, invoking for reader or audience sacred associations, and a heightened sense of con-vention, of propriety in behaviour and language. The Friar strengthens these responses by quoting from the Marriage Service itself:

*Friar.* If either of you know any inward impediment why you should not be conjoined, I charge you on your souls to utter it. (IV. i. 11-13)

It is in such a context as this that Claudio's accusation is uttered, and in which it makes such a powerful impact. Our sense of occasion, of propriety and decorum is outraged; the violence of Claudio's language, in this hushed setting, causes horrified shock:

*Claudio.* ... But you are more intemperate in your blood
        Than Venus, or those pamp'red animals
        That rage in savage sensuality.(IV. i. 58–60)

It is not so much that we feel for Hero as an individual—we know very little about her—but we respond with acute pain to this abrupt and even savage denial of marriage; here, on the very brink of the ceremony itself, in church. The whole play has been gathering towards the goal of wedlock—Claudio and Hero betrothed in the opening act, Benedick just gone off-stage to ask Beatrice's father for her hand—and now the whole edifice lies apparently wrecked. We have been conditioned to thinking of the comedy as working towards the confirmation of happiness in marriage (Don John's machinations have seemed idle threats) so that we respond to this crisis with an appropriate degree of shock. The shock, certainly, that the crises of melodrama bring; the contrived setting, the exaggeration of the language, the incredible promptitude with which Hero 'dies' all advise us of the appropriate provisional, half-detached response. But for the moment it takes our breath away.

After the accusation itself, attention is directed towards Hero's father and her uncle. If we rarely find adequate discussion of the early part of the scene, discussion of the two old men's grief is even more infrequent. And yet the central part of the 'Church' scene and the opening of Act V are concerned at some considerable length with Leonato's grief and Antonio's. Nor is it a matter of length only; the language employed is under a pressure of emotion and displays a metaphorical suggestiveness that marks it off from the common run of verse in this play. A critical reading of the text cannot afford to ignore lines such as these, to take a single example:

*Leonato.* ... Why ever wast thou lovely in my eyes?
        Why had I not with charitable hand
        Took up a beggar's issue at my gates,
        Who smirchèd thus and mired with infamy,
        I might have said, "No part of it is mine;
        This shame derives itself from unknown loins"?

> But mine, and mine I loved, and mine I praised,
> And mine that I was proud on, mine so much
> That I myself was to myself not mine,
> Valuing of her—why she, O, she is fall'n
> Into a pit of ink, that the wide sea
> Hath drops too few to wash her clean again,
> And salt too little which may season give
> To her foul tainted flesh! (IV. i. 129-42)

This is, certainly, transitional verse; the lines that play with 'mine' are reminiscent of the early sonnets or of parts of *Richard II* rather than the verse of Shakespeare's maturity. But the rhetorical drive, the economy of means in the early lines are unmistakably the work of a poet in full command of his medium; and of one who would wish the subject treated given due weight in performance or reading. Even the 'mine' sequence of thought has in its iteration an appropriateness to the distraught repetitiveness of deep grief. And the metaphors of 'tainted flesh', 'the wide sea' and 'cleansing' do not recall several of Shakespeare's greatest plays (notably of course *Macbeth* and *Hamlet*) merely by chance. For Shakespeare is here allowing this play to ride as close as he dare to the borders of tragedy; and his purpose evokes the appropriate language. If we are to appreciate the full richness of the *Much Ado* experience we must be prepared to give due emphasis to this 'tragic' aspect; no other comedy embraces anything like such a range of emotional states, from the wholly carefree to the desperately grieved.

At the risk of causing an imbalance in our response, we ought to notice in a little detail the other scene in which Leonato's grief and Antonio's is conveyed. Act V scene i confronts us with a problem of response: is the opening sequence of this scene written to extend the experience of deep dismay in which the Church scene deals, and to hint at further possibilities of evil as Don Pedro and Claudio are challenged to a duel by Antonio and Leonato; or is it intended to provide local comic effect as two old dotards, unhinged by grief, utter they know not what? The scene is often played as though the second were Shakespeare's (or perhaps one should say the play's) intention; and the opening scene of Act II would seem to support this attitude. For there Antonio is very evidently characterised, during the masked dance, as an inept old man, a conventional portrait of old age, provocative of laughter only (see II. i. 111-23). Is the actor to present, then, a consistent portrait, and behave here in Act V with parallel absurdity? If he does so, the strong possibility arises that this whole portion of the scene will slide into farce, making the challenge to Don Pedro and Claudio ludicrous, and reflecting back undermining laughter on Leonato's protestations of grief at his daughter's disgrace. Carefully critical reading is necessary to determine which way performance ought to turn.

Some of Antonio's lines clearly suggest that he loses self-control; his utterance at lines 8off. is that of an over-excited, incompetent old man, quite unfitted to challenge the confident, reserved Don Pedro (the physical contrast between the two men, on the stage or in the mind's eye, will enforce the contrast):

*Antonio.* He shall kill two of us, and men indeed.
        But that's no matter; let him kill one first.
        Win me and wear me! Let him answer me.
        Come, follow me, boy; come, sir boy; come, follow me.
        Sir boy, I'll whip you from your foining fence!
        Nay, as I am a gentleman, I will (V. i. 80-85)

These are the accents of an ultra-Polonius. And yet we ought to hesitate before we play them for laughter. Because they may equally well be evidence of a mind near the borders of sanity, uncomprehending of the probabilities understood by a mind less disturbed, since a single grief has occupied and controlled all its faculties. That this is a more fitting interpretation is suggested by the verse Shakespeare gives Leonato, Antonio's partner in grief. His opening speeches contain some of the play's most forceful dramatic poetry:

*Leonato.* I pray thee cease thy counsel,
        Which falls into mine ears as profitless
        As water in a sieve. Give not me counsel,
        Nor let no comforter delight mine ear
        But such a one whose wrongs do suit with mine.
        Bring me a father that so loved his child,
        Whose joy of her is overwhelmed like mine,
        And bid him speak of patience. . . .
        I pray thee peace. I will be flesh and blood;
        For there was never yet philosopher
        That could endure the toothache patiently,
        However they have writ the style of gods
        And made a push at chance and sufferance. (V. i. 3-38)

We have here a sorrow that is intended to strike us as pitiably real; the language of these and the omitted speeches testifies eloquently to that. The mixture of unaffected simplicity and metaphoric (here almost allegoric) strength, together with the lithe aphorism that caps the argument, bespeak a perfectly serious intention, one realised with all the verbal means at the author's command. It would seem mere wilfulness to risk diluting the reality of Leonato's grief by placing it side-by-side with absurdity. With pathetic incomprehension, perhaps. We cannot on a sensitive reading agree to a laughter-provoking rôle for Antonio: the full gravity of the opening section of Act V must be appreciated.

As we have seen, then, the first two movements take us through gaiety and sorrow—'joy could not show itself modest [moderate, fitting] enough without a badge of bitterness.' The non-responsible light-heartedness associated with Benedick and Beatrice, careless of 'chance and sufferance', has modulated into the grave emotions of the Church scene and after. Thus Shakespeare has contoured the affective 'shape' of the play, and set up conflicting emotions. Now he proposes what we have called a 'resolution'. Again, to a visually unreceptive reading, this resolution may seem peculiarly lightweight and inconsequential, a forced and hurried ending. But in the theatre, or on visualised reading, it can have the effect of a real conclusion, the establishment of a new and more permanent happiness; much as a full close in music, with every discord resolved.

The final movement begins (though it has important links stretching backwards) with the action at 'Hero's tomb' (V. iii.). We have already commented on the impressive emotional experience to which the action before the tomb properly gives rise, the sense of an exhausted darkness, as the black-dressed mourners and musicians speak and chant. But in the following lines a contrary impulse manifests itself; there supervenes a passage that brings with it opposite ideas, the springing of new life and new purposes:

*Don Pedro.*  Good morrow, masters; put your torches out.
            The wolves have preyed, and look, the gentle day,
            Before the wheels of Phoebus, round about
            Dapples the drowsy east with spots of gray.
            Thanks to you all, and leave us. Fare you well (V. iii. 24-28)

The delicate lyric grace of these lines sets them apart from everything else in the play; spoken by a gifted actor, their cadence alone sufficiently informs us that an important turning-point in the action has arrived. The lyric note hints that less burdensome experience will follow, and this the language used confirms. The emphasis falls on images of sunrise and morning; the darkness in which evil thrived (the wolf-image) is over, and morning comes with its new life and freedom. The famous lines that follow the departure of the Ghost in *Hamlet* ('But, look, the morn in russet mantle clad . . ') carry the same message of assurance after the terror of the night (though in that play the day's purposes may seem clearer than they are). Here Shakespeare goes on to underline the promise of the new day by referring specifically to the fresh and brighter clothes his actors will wear when they next appear:

*Don Pedro.* Come, let us hence and put on other weeds,
           And then to Leonato's we will go. (V. iii. 30-31)

In the theatre, the visual contrast between the 'tomb' scene and the final scene at Leonato's house (V. iv.) would be very marked. Already, on the modern stage, intensifying light would imitate the dawning of a new day, a new day of theatrical experience as well as in the play's time-scheme; on both Elizabethan and modern stages gesture and movement would give the effect of new freedom—the play has shaken off the grave restraints of its second movement. Altogether, the change-over is an impressive theatrical experience; assuring us, despite what has occurred, of the confirmed happiness in which the comedy will end.

The, as yet, muted promise of the 'tomb' scene bears fruit in the full morning that succeeds it. Amid the chatter and movement of Leonato's house, (note that 'good morrow' is repeated four times between ll. 34 and 40), Shakespeare invokes an even more powerful symbolism than the morning-and-new-clothes we have just been discussing. The 're-birth' or 'resurrection' of Hero carries further, in terms familiar to the Elizabethans, and not entirely obscure to a modern reader, themes of new life and innocence:

*Claudio.*    Give me your hand; before this holy friar
              I am your husband if you like of me.
*Hero.*       And when I lived I was your other wife; [*unmasking*]
              And when you loved you were my other husband.
*Claudio.*    Another Hero!
*Hero.*                  Nothing certainer.
              One Hero died defiled; but I do live,
              And surely as I live, I am a maid.

*Don Pedro.* The former Hero! Hero that is dead!
*Leonato.*        She died, my lord, but whiles her slander lived. (V. iv.
            58-66)

This is the final confirmation of the comic experience the play exists
to communicate. The 'death' that Don John's slander brought with it—
the grievous experience of the second movement—has been cancelled by
the re-birth of happiness, a happiness the comic form bids us take as
permanent.

*Much Ado* closes with a dance. It is devised, says Benedick 'that we
may lighten our own hearts and our wives' heels'. But an Elizabethan
audience would have discerned wider meanings in it than this; and even
we, as we visualise each actor taking his part in the graceful, *orderly*,
steps, his every movement perfectly allied to his fellows' movements and
the whole governed by music, can without difficulty appreciate the
dance as symbol of order. (Consider how we still use such words as
'concord' 'harmony' 'attuned', each a dead metaphor from music).
Beatrice has already (II. i. 68-79) briefly and delightfully parodied Sir
John Davies' *Orchestra; A Poem of Dancing* (1596), a very well known
work which uses the dance as symbol of order, on personal, political
and indeed universal levels. Clearly, an early audience would have seen
the concluding dance as a satisfactory symbol of the happiness-confirm-
ing order with which comedy leaves us. As marriage itself is a symbol
of order, society's divinely-sanctioned means of controlling and directing
sexual relations. About this the Elizabethan homilists are explicit.
Shakespeare and his audience would have regarded the marriage with
which each of his comedies ends as more than a convenient stopping-
place or as a 'romantic' (in its modern, debased sense) convenience; they
take their place as the fitting resolution of the diverse experience in
which each play has dealt.

So the play has moved through gaiety and woe on to confirmed
happiness: love begun, love challenged and love triumphant in marriage.
For an audience or reader the experience is one of 'pleasurable reassurance'—a demonstration in terms of theatre that good will conquer, that
'all shall be well'. So it is with all Shakespeare's comedies before, say,
1601 (the 'early' and 'mature' but not the 'problem' nor of course 'the
last'). All are 'happy' (Dover Wilson's word) in the sense that they deal
vivaciously with their subjects, and all display an almost total absence of
severe judgements. Exceptions do of course exist: Shylock, for example,

and Malvolio are treated with clear disapproval, as is Don John in the present play. And yet *Much Ado* is characteristic in focusing attention at the end elsewhere than on the villain:

*Messenger.* My lord, your brother John is ta'en in flight,
            And brought with armèd men back to Messina.
*Benedick.* Think not on him till tomorrow. I'll devise thee brave
            punishments for him. Strike up, pipers!

The philosophy behind these plays involves, as the final speech suggests, the belief that evil can be excluded and punished, and without having first caused irreparable damage to the society on which it was parasitic.

# 3. *Character in Action*

So far, we have been content to discuss *Much Ado* as though we were talking, in a non-technical way, about a piece of music. The opening movement, we have in effect been saying, comprises a vivacious *allegro* in a major key, the second a slow minor, and the third (once more in a major key) a full, if brief, resolution. But the musical analogy is only of limited helpfulness when discussing literature; for literature offers not only broad emotional impressions but also interests of a different order. A valid response involves for example our moral and ethical attitudes in a way music never asks. And so we must go on from talking about the general emotional graph of *Much Ado* to asking questions about the main characters and their experience within the play. What sort of people are they? Do they develop during the course of the action? Does their experience rehearse, and so imaginatively validate, any general or particular moral lessons? These are the questions literature naturally leads us to ask; more particularly *dramatic* literature, for the presence of the actor on stage almost inevitably leads us to ask questions about personality, just as we do (in reflection at least) about our acquaintances of everyday. Character-analysis and moral questioning may play little part in our reading of some literary forms, but they are almost inescapable in the theatre.

We must however be careful. Sensitive reading of a play-text, as of any literature, involves prominently a delicate sense of proportion. We must not only know the appropriate questions to ask; we must also know precisely how far to press them, and how major a place to give the answers in the total experience of the play. With Shakespearean tragedy (and to an extent history) we may sometimes question character minutely, and offer our conclusions as a major part of the play-experience; *Hamlet* and *Othello* become richer the more closely we question the character and moral behaviour of the hero. (Though even in these plays we must always remind ourselves that the characters are formed and defined by the literary, not the real, world.) *Lear* and *Macbeth* reward close moral questioning less richly. But even they give more substantially in this direction than the comedies. In tragedy, meaning usually clusters round the life-experience of a single hero; in comedy no character enjoys similar prominence, but is one figure only in the crowded pattern. And so a comedy cannot explore any individual's personality and behaviour in rich detail; and we must not attempt to construct out of our reading elaborate psychological portraits. Nor should we expect profound moral issues to be explored; such exploration is possible only in the presence of detailed and subtle characterisation. The characters of comedy, we will find, are token portaits only, and their development is signified rather than richly investigated. We must expect no more than a moral paradigm; and accord it proportional place in the total literary and theatrical experience.

Claudio and Hero are the characters of the nominal main plot. Shakespeare found the figures who suggested them and their experience in his (probable) sources, Ariosto's *Orlando Furioso* (translated by Sir John Harington) and Bandello's *Novelle* (perhaps in Belleforest's French). And yet even a casual reading of *Much Ado* shows that the major part of his creative energy went into forming Beatrice and Benedick. In a sense these figures, like Claudio and Hero, are not original with Shakespeare; sixteenth century English and Continental literature provides many earlier examples of mutually-derisive 'lovers'. But it was Shakespeare's deliberate choice, or inspiration, to graft such a pair, with their typical antagonism-become-love experience, into the old stock of the Claudio and Hero tale. The chances are, therefore, that their experience may reflect even more clearly than the derived main plot some moral paradigm Shakespeare wished to convey. And so we may usefully begin by questioning what their attitudes are, and how these develop in the course of the action.

Nothing is gained by considering the two separately; from the opening scene they are voices in concert. Beatrice may be the more redoubtable opponent; in the 'masked ball' scene she so dismays Benedick that he begs Don Pedro with comic exaggeration to 'commend [him] any service to the world's end' rather than ask him to 'hold three words' conference with this harpy'. But by and large they are such notable antagonists because they are so evenly matched; in terms they might themselves accept, they play the same game and they play it equally well.

Our response to the early Beatrice and Benedick consists very largely in marvelling at their sheer vitality. We delight in their high spirits, admire their vigorous debunking sanity and are swept away by their sheer verbal and logical resource. Their wit is endlessly inventive; on the flimsiest basis they can erect the most baroquely-decorated structures of mock logic. The zest with which Beatrice tackles the concept 'husband' is exhilarating:

*Leonato.* Well, niece, I hope to see you one day fitted with a husband.
*Beatrice.* Not till God make men of some other metal than earth. Would it not grieve a woman to be overmastered with a piece of valiant dust? To make an account of her life to a clod of wayward marl? No, uncle, I'll none. Adam's sons are my brethren, and truly I hold it a sin to match in my kindred. (II. i. 57-64)

The essence of this is a masterful contortion of accepted commonplace; dead metaphor and cliché are shaken into new and unfamiliar life. And this is typical; Benedick appropriately remarks on another occasion how Beatrice has 'frightened the word of his right sense, so forcible is [her] wit' (V. ii. 55-6). It is this *force* we acknowledge. Neither Beatrice's wit nor Benedick's has the Falstaffian breadth of humour, its abundant warmth; in *Much Ado* the mirth is far more intellectual, has more to do with mental agility, a narrow and intense cleverness. But it does have the Falstaffian resource; and to this, its essential and apparently inexhaustible vitality, we delightedly respond. For the first three acts Beatrice and Benedick are the incarnation of this wit, and we transfer to them as characters the delight we take in their words.

And yet we must sometimes feel, even if in some rather distant corner of our consciousness, that what they say (and therefore what they are) in these first acts cannot be unreservedly accepted. Because they work against the whole positive drive of the play. We know of course that they will be 'converted' (Hero's word at III. iv. 88) from mockers of love into love's thralls; this is the traditional pattern they exemplify and one we can predict from the beginning. But Shakespeare is not content to make this 'conversion' a mere narrative matter only; it becomes the vehicle of a moral paradigm. They are converted in fact from an unacceptable moral stance to one we can fully endorse.

There are hints in the early scenes that Beatrice's attitude will not do. Benedick, in his sharply perceptive way, calls her 'my dear Lady Disdain' (I. i. 114), and Leonato describes her as 'too curst' (II. i. 20); despite Beatrice's clever replies these labels stick. But it is in the garden scene, when Beatrice hears from concealment the talk between Hero and

Margaret, that Shakespeare makes his moral points with the greatest firmness:

*Hero.* O god of love! I know he doth deserve
As much as may be yielded to a man;
But Nature never framed a woman's heart
Of prouder stuff than that of Beatrice.
Disdain and Scorn ride sparkling in her eyes,
Misprizing what they look on; and her wit
Values itself so highly that to her
All matter else seems weak. She cannot love,
Nor take no shape nor project of affection,
She is so self-endeared. (III. i. 47-56)

The terms may be taken as exaggerated, intended as they are for over-hearing. But the indictment is essentially just; and serious. Beatrice is characterised as the embodiment of pride; her 'disdain' and 'scorn' distort and denature every experience that comes under her notice; her wit is autotelic, regardful of nothing but its own brilliance. Above all, she *cannot love* because the focus of her attention is herself. It requires no very profound knowledge of Shakespeare's work to recognise that he is here describing a crippled personality, the very antithesis of the outgoing, self-giving character he values most highly. And her inclinations at this stage of the play run counter to what H. B. Charlton has described as the basis of 'lasting happiness' in the comedies: 'the gift of intuitive sympathy, and the habit of forbearance and of tolerance.'

Benedick is less severely treated in the parallel scene (II. iii.); perhaps because his wit is that degree less caustic. But both he and Beatrice, in soliloquy, agree to put their faults to mending. Both reject pride:

*Beatrice.* [*Coming forward*] What fire is in mine ears?
Can this be true?
Stand I condemned for pride and scorn so much?
Contempt, farewell! And maiden pride, adieu!
No glory lives behind the back of such. (III. i. 107-10)

*Benedick.* Love me? Why, it must be requited. I hear how I am censured. They say I will bear myself proudly if I perceive the love come from her. They say too that she will rather die than give any sign of affection. I did never think to marry; I must not seem proud. Happy are they that hear their detractions and can put them to mending. (II. iii. 220-26)

It is out of these resolves to banish pride that (after a comic anticipation on Benedick's part) they create a mutual awareness; self-regard turns in other words into love. The scene of their mutual acknowledgement (IV. i.) is among the most moving in the play, and must clearly be regarded as a climax of the action. Where they had previously delighted to offend and score off each other, they now approach with a delicacy and half-embarrassed reticence that bespeaks an altogether new awareness. The moment of declaration can in the theatre be immensely telling:

*Benedick.*  I do love nothing in the world so well as you. Is not that strange? . . .
*Beatrice.*  You have stayed me in a happy hour. I was about to protest I loved you.
*Benedick.*  And do it with all thy heart.
*Beatrice.*  I love you with so much of my heart that none is left to protest. (IV. i. 266-85)

These are the accents of complete mutuality. How total a 'conversion' this new attitude represents for both of them needs no emphasis; reciprocal affection has altogether taken the place of the self-regardful wit that had been their dominant, shared, characteristic. In the token terms in which comedy deals a new moral position has been established, and one to which we may react with positive acceptance.

The structure of the moral paradigm is so far clear. Wit and its attendant qualities of scorn and pride have given way to the mutuality of love. Quite obviously, this is a point of achievement, for in all these plays love, as we said at the outset, is the measure of moral good. Yet the 'conversion' of Beatrice and Benedick has not yet been locked into the general pattern of *Much Ado*; for that pattern includes, as we have seen, 'bitterness' as well as 'joy'. Overhearing their faults discussed certainly holds for such a proud, self-centred pair a measure of bitterness; and each has had to undergo (in III. ii. and III. iv.) the flouting due to them as love's mockers become love's thralls. But the temper of all these episodes is that characteristic of the play's first movement: almost undiluted levity. Neither of the pair has yet participated substantially in the grief-conscious experience that typifies the second movement. And until their relationship has been exposed to such experience they cannot be said to have entered fully into the *Much Ado* world, nor can they share in the *confirmed* happiness with which the play ends.

Immediately after their mutual acknowledgement Shakespeare allows

Don John's malice, or its results, to impinge upon them too. Benedick protests, in the spirit of their new mutuality:

> Come, bid me do anything for thee.

Beatrice's reply is devastating:

> Kill Claudio.

A reader or audience is shocked, as Benedick is shocked. He had not anticipated that the claims of love could extend quite so far into the territory of bitterness. But Beatrice insists: the love he offers cannot be adequate until he has so espoused Hero's grief, has so identified himself with the new grief-conscious temper of the play, that he will do what he can to amend it. Even if that requires the killing of his closest friend. Beatrice exemplifies with withering contempt one who would fail to reach the standard she sets; the characteristics advanced are worth notice:

> O that I were a man for his sake! Or that I had any friend would be a man for my sake! But manhood is melted into curtsies, valor into compliment, and men are only turned into tongue, and trim ones too. He is now as valiant as Hercules that only tells a lie, and swears it (IV. i. 313-20)

'Men are only turned into tongue': Benedick had been merely a voice, even if a magnificently active one, in the early scenes. Now he is challenged to become 'a man'.

Benedick hesitates only long enough to be certain that Beatrice believes what she has been saying 'in her soul' (i.e. not only on the level of fancy) before espousing the new seriousness required of him. When he next appears, he is a new personality. Claudio and Don Pedro have just daffed aside the challenges cast at them by Leonato and Antonio, and expect the carefree Benedick of old to amuse them. But his new attitude shows itself at once:

> In a false quarrel there is no true valor. (V. i. 120)

Light-hearted travesty, his usual mode, is here replaced by earnestness. But he is embarrassed by his reputation, and so must insist on his new position; he does so by scourging wit:

> Sir your wit ambles well; it goes easily. (V. i. 157)

He is not amused by a discourse on how Beatrice mocked his own wit (notice how Shakespeare keeps that topic before us); with his new status as 'a man' he can berate Claudio ('boy') in the most high-handed manner:

> Fare you well, boy; you know my mind. I will leave you now to your gossiplike humor; you break jests as braggards do their blades, which God be thanked hurt not. (V. i. 183-86)

This altogether more serious frame of mind gradually makes itself felt; in the theatre the changing, and dismayed, expressions of Claudio and Don Pedro suggest and reflect the audience's awareness that a new term has been added to the paradigm of Benedick's moral experience. Claudio speaks perhaps more truly than he knows when he seeks to explain this altered Benedick:

*Don Pedro.*  He is in earnest.
*Claudio.*    In most profound earnest; and, I'll warrant you, for the love of Beatrice. (V. i. 193-5)

The love of Beatrice is being earned during this scene.

Under the comic hypothesis, the challenge never issues in a duel: 'all shall be well'. To have allowed one to occur over such a serious issue (contrast the Viola-Sir Andrew 'duel' in *Twelfth Night*) would have edged the play into the genre of tragicomedy. Shakespeare uses Dogberry and Verges to prevent any such outcome. But by the threat of actual conflict (and we are never quite sure it will not materialise) the necessary end has been achieved: the Beatrice and Benedick relationship has been brought substantially within the grave temper of the play's second movement. To mutuality has been added the confirmation that comes with meeting and overcoming the challenge of serious issues.

Beatrice and Benedick have one further brief encounter (V. ii.) before the final scene discovers all and double marriage symbolises the establishment of lasting happiness. On both occasions the pair evince once more high spirits; it was no part of Shakespeare's (or rather the comedy's) philosophy that love should produce dullards. Once again wit comes into play; but not now a wit that seeks its own advantage and distorts every subject it touches. Each of the two now delights in the other's agility of mind, and acknowledges that delight. The whole dialogue at V. ii. 55ff. is of this character. And the final scene too, despite the pair's unwillingness to capitulate publicly, represents mutual conquest. Benedick closes the exchange appropriately:

Peace! I will stop your mouth. (V. iv. 97)

The conventional retort, prelude to a kiss, has here the force of the whole play behind it: words have been love's antagonists, and are now at love's triumph silenced by a kiss.

The complete paradigm of the love-experience of Beatrice and Benedick is now before us. From the proud self-centred antagonists who domineered over experience and sought to wound each other, the pair developed into mutually self-giving lovers; and the validity of their love then extended to involving themselves in the grief that fell on Hero and on her friends. In the course of the play they are, in other words, educated into a fully valid love, tested under adversity and then confirmed in marriage. Remembering the references to becoming 'a man' one might describe this as a process of maturation; we cannot doubt that at the end Beatrice and Benedick are fuller individuals (or signify fuller individuals) than at the beginning.

It is at this point that we have to ask questions about the place of moral development within the total meaning of the play. In the summary just given we have discussed our moral paradigm as though that were the single concern of the unfolding narrative. Such a procedure is forced on the critic by the discursive method he must employ. We ought, however, to be careful to replace the analysed experience in the context of theatre, with its multitude of simultaneous impressions. Otherwise we give it a prominence quite unnatural when checked against performance or sensitive reading. In particular, we must recall a theatre-performance's overriding humour; without question this is the gayest of Shakespeare's comedies (in its first movement, that is). To take the twin 'garden' scenes as an example, there can be no doubt that the dominant experience in the theatre—whatever moral developments are taking place—is one of sheer delight in the duping of Beatrice and Benedick and amusement at the deceivers' cleverness. Given a moderately inventive performance, an audience will rock with laughter. But we ought not, either, to make the opposite error; and suppose that because we laugh we cannot also be conscious of moral issues. The human mind is capable of registering more than a single impression at any one time—especially when the impressions are mutually illuminating, as here. Besides the exhilaration and

life-enhancing zest of comedy, the 'pleasurable reassurance' we talked of
in the previous section, we can register a moral development such as we
have just been discussing. It may not be the dominant, immediate, factor
in watching or reading *Much Ado* (and we ought to adjust our criticism
if we make it seem otherwise), but it is certainly *there*, a vital factor, to
complement other interests and enrich the general comic experience.

If the sub-plot's moral paradigm is less than blatant, it is at any rate
clear and unquestionable once it has been exposed and discussed. The
way in which it strengthens the dominant narrative line (love's mockers
become love's thralls) requires little urging. The situation in the main
plot is a little different. There, what we shall offer as moral paradigm is
less fully developed, and depends to a certain extent on snapping up
trifles that will only become felt experience when the actor gives them
substantial body in the theatre. The actor of Claudio, that is: Hero is
little more than a passive figure upon whom events play.

Before, however, we can elicit the nature of Claudio's experience,
and ask questions about any moral 'education' with which we might
credit him, we shall have to face a considerable problem. Readers and
critics often express their more or less strong distaste for him. Andrew
Lang's 'a hateful young cub', repeated with variation by others, is one
of the milder phrases to be met with. The consequences are obvious: if
we dislike Claudio we can hardly respond enthusiastically to his union
with Hero. Indeed the whole main plot will become the confirmation
of a morally unacceptable relationship; we greet the last scene's marriage
with protest, not acclaim. And this could not be described as the securest
ground on which to build moral argument.

The 'Church' scene often causes the major difficulty. To accuse Hero
in such a setting, on such an occasion and before such a company—her
father, her friends, her servants—seems the act of a callous monster. And
indeed we would have to agree that the temperament which permitted
this scene had in it an element of (to be non-commital) coldness. When
Don John suggested Hero's unchastity, Claudio failed to spring to her
defence; rather the present occasion immediately framed itself in his
imagination:

*Claudio.* If I see anything tonight why I should not marry her tomorrow, in the congregation where I should wed, there will
I shame her. (III. ii. 119-21)

Beatrice's warmth finds this infamous (IV. i. 299ff.). Yet we would be guilty of insensitive reading if we gave too much weight either to Claudio's anticipation, or to the circumstances of the Church scene itself. The necessity for those circumstances we have already explained; at this juncture in the action Shakespeare required a scene capable of putting across, with intense theatrical force, a sense of crisis, the break-down of an apparently unassailable progress towards marriage. Hence his choice of an overtly 'theatrical' setting; for the play's purposes, the denunciation *had* to be in Church—private and restrained accusation could not have carried the necessary force. And Claudio's anticipation is the dramatist's way of preparing our expectations for this crucial scene. Once it has arrived, our anxieties focus on the success of Don John's malice, and on Hero's misfortune. We concentrate but little on what reflection or leisured reading might tell us to be Claudio's and (it should not be forgotten) Don Pedro's want of delicacy; if we think of them at all, we regard them as more sinned against than sinning—they are Don John's victims much more than Hero theirs. To dwell on Claudio's callousness, in other words, is to fail in sensitivity to the play's appro-priate theatrical requirements.

But there are other objections to Claudio not so easily dislodged. These centre round the assertion that he is an impossibly *unromantic* figure. Modern taste demands that the hero of love-narrative perform certain ritual gestures towards his proposed conquest, that he engage in deeply emotional (and for preference painful) wooing, and that he refrain from hard-headed discussion of social or financial practicalities. A very little reflection on the events of *Much Ado* will show that on all counts Claudio is a dismal failure. With the result that a modern audience finds it singularly difficult to see him as in any sense a lover, and hence tends to resist acceptance of his ultimate marriage. It is here that C. T. Prouty's work on the sources of *Much Ado* may prove helpful. One way out of the *impasse* is to argue that Shakespeare did not *intend* us to think of Claudio as being 'in love' in the romantic sense of the phrase; and this way Prouty takes. He notes, to begin with, that *Much Ado* contrasts with all earlier versions of the Claudio-Hero tale (or at any rate with all those in which the Hero and Claudio figures are extensively treated) in that Shakespeare refuses to Claudio the behaviour of a conventional Elizabethan lover. In contrast to previous 'Claudios', he sends no impassioned love-letters, writes no exaggerated sonnets (as Benedick

does, and Orlando of *As You Like It*); he offers no rapturous description of his mistress' person, nor recounts how powerfully he has been
affected by contemplation of her beauty (his dialogue with Don Pedro in
I. i. is tentative in the extreme); he suffers no love-sickness. The absence
of all these traits, together with Claudio's extraordinary detachment
almost throughout is inconsistent, as Prouty notes, with the expectations
of Romantic love. And more, Claudio violates those expectations by
refusing even to do his own wooing; his asking Don Pedro to engage
the girl for him, and thus to involve himself substantially in the affair,
would be anathema to any serious Romantic. And yet, Prouty points
out, such behaviour would be entirely acceptable, indeed correct, for
anyone wishing to achieve another type of marriage-relationship, and
one very familiar at all levels of Elizabethan society: the 'arranged
marriage' or *mariage de covenance*. Under this, emotions mattered little;
what counted was social compatibility and financial advantage. There
were no 'halting sonnets' to be written, no love-sicknesses to be endured.
Only a dowry arranged—normally with the assistance of a senior friend
or parent—and troths plighted. Which is, Prouty suggests, precisely
Claudio's aim and achievement.

   *Much Ado* lends this contention a great deal of support. (Don John's
instinct to address, not Claudio, but Don Pedro when he wishes to accuse
Hero should be pondered—III. ii. 76ff.) From Prouty's argument it is
clear that Shakespeare had the customs of the *mariage de covenance* much
in mind when writing Claudio's part. Any of his first audience would
have recognised and accepted without protest the standard forms of
behaviour. And what the Elizabethan would have found perfectly natural
and perfectly acceptable in Claudio—his 'unromantic' ways—ought quite
obviously not to prevent *us* responding sympathetically towards him.
We ought to adjust our more romantically-inclined notions until we
can feel with an Elizabethan audience on these points. If Claudio invites
Don Pedro to do his wooing for him, and thinks often thereafter in terms
of a marriage-bargain, sealed and signed through his friend's agency, we
must not protest.

   The *mariage de covenance* explanation does indeed dislodge some
objections to Claudio. But it raises problems also, if it asks us to understand Claudio's experience in the play merely as the successful prosecu-
tion of a business venture. To begin with, the betrothal of Claudio
and Hero (whatever we say about Claudio's initial broaching of the

affair to Benedick and Don Pedro) speaks a language that is distinct from the idiom of commerce:

*Claudio.*  Silence is the perfectest herald of joy. I were but little happy if I could say how much. Lady, as you are mine, I am yours. I give away myself for you and dote upon the exchange. (II. i. 303-6)

This is the language of reciprocated feeling. Commerce involves acquisition, it does not allow for self-giving. Quite evidently we are not invited to think here of a relationship that rests on a narrowly commercial basis; it involves the mutuality of love. And we have eloquent testimony from Benedick at the beginning of II. iii. that Claudio ('Monsieur Love') has surrendered himself to the claims of feeling. Benedick's typical exaggeration and invention are no doubt responsible for placing his friend so far in the realms of convention; Claudio in actuality betrays none of the caricatured features Benedick plays upon (and it is important for our argument that he should not). And yet Benedick's portrait rightly affects our estimate of Claudio's experience. More important than either of these, all our instincts, nourished on a reading of Shakespeare's other work, and particularly the other mature comedies, reject a hypothesis as simple as Prouty's. H. B. Charlton describes the essential focus of the comedies as 'the problem and the opportunity by which man's destiny was most richly to be realised—his aptitude for the disciplinary experiences of love'. Very little 'disciplinary experience' of this order could, even arguably, come out of the completion of a marriage-bargain; and whatever its distinctive features, we take *Much Ado* to be one in spirit with the other comedies of the group. As the play gathers towards marriage, and then is thwarted, we feel that serious issues are involved—more serious, certainly, than commercial success and failure. Don John's malice threatens a whole edifice of personal and social values, and not just the aspirations of a young fortune-hunter. If we believe otherwise, the play becomes trifling indeed.

How then are we to combine Prouty's findings with the belief that *Much Ado* has in hand weightier matters than commerce? If we speculate, in attempting an answer, on Shakespeare's 'intentions' prior to writing the play, it must not be thought that we can infer these from *Much Ado*; we have the completed work of art and that is all. But such speculation, while illegitimate, does provide a useful strategy for exploring the intrinsic 'meaning' of the main plot; and we may, guardedly, make use of it.

Our theory might run like this. Shakespeare's mature comedies all submit various briefly-created types of personality to the 'disciplinary experiences of love'. (Consideration of, for example, *As You Like It* or *Twelfth Night* will quickly confirm this.) It may be that he now sought to construct a play in which one rather extreme personality-type— which particular type we shall see in a moment—might be exposed to such experience, and that type one that would find the *mariage de covenance* procedures congenial. (We must again remind ourselves that neither Shakespeare nor his original audience would find anything shameful or weak in this.) The old Claudio-Hero tale may have seemed to lend a framework for this aim; provided it was altered in such a way as to exclude the distinctive features of Romance—as Prouty tells us actually happened. But adoption of the *procedures* of the arranged marriage would not exclude for Shakespeare, as it should not for us, the sense that Claudio was engaging in an experience of the utmost consequence; the distinction is merely between our demanding the trappings of Romance, while Shakespeare's contemporaries did not. The type of personality Shakespeare had in mind dictated the mode of wooing. So he imagined Claudio, and exposed him to the events of the *Much Ado* narrative, with the intention of using him as yet another 'controlled experiment' in the investigation of how 'the disciplinary experiences of love' 'educate' various types of personality. We can at least put our theory in these terms, while remaining conscious that its language is far too flat and deliberate to be apt to what actually happened; what we attribute to conscious intention took place in that 'quick forge and working-house of thought', Shakespeare's creative imagination.

To corroborate our ideas we shall have to analyse Claudio's personality. And this should lead us in turn to an understanding of the moral paradigm to which his experience gives definition.

An actor playing Claudio will find the part one of the most consistently drawn in Shakespeare's comedies. While it cannot, as we have said, share the depth of one of the major portraits in tragedy, it does to some extent anticipate these, for it is the skeleton of a fully credible personality—more so than any other figure in *Much Ado*, even Beatrice —well enough articulated for the actor to create from it a convincing stage-portrait. The several contributing facets are merely sketched-in, but they interlock very suggestively. We may draw attention to the three major among them.

Our first impressions of Claudio, even before he is himself on stage, set him in direct contrast to Benedick. We hear Benedick talked of as 'Cupid's adversary', as 'a very valiant trencher-man', as one 'pleasant [i.e. lively] as ever he was'; whether these phrases are worded by friend or adversary (and Beatrice's position is of course equivocal) they speak of a 'good fellow', an entertaining, voluble companion. Claudio we hear of very differently. The Messenger speaks of him as one who 'hath borne himself beyond the promise of his age, doing, in the figure of a lamb, the feats of a lion'; at a loss for terms sufficiently high-sounding, he assures us Claudio 'hath indeed better bett'red expectation than you must expect of me to tell you how' (I. i. 13-17). Whatever these phrases owe to a Messenger's proper officialese, they prepare us for finding 'the right noble Claudio' (Beatrice's faintly ironic words) a man appropriately spoken of in such conventionalities. And this is what he proves: beside the richly various, unpredictable Benedick, he is a sober, dull-tinted and altogether conformist figure. As the play develops he becomes more and more Benedick's anti-type: sober where the other is the embodiment of gaiety, level-headed as against rash, one who treats language in the most measured respectful way as compared with the other's marvellous extravagances. His conformism shows itself above all in the astonishingly equable demeanour he preserves in almost all the play's crises; apart from momentary excitement in the Church scene ('those pamp'red animals, That rage in savage sensuality') and a reflex gesture of the hand towards his sword to meet Leonato's challenge, he is everywhere in complete control of his feelings. In an immediately cognate way, his reactions altogether lack spirit; when persuaded he has lost Hero to Don Pedro he evinces nothing more than the dejection of 'a poor hurt fowl' (II. i. 200). For all these related symptoms Beatrice supplies the appropriate word:

> The Count is neither sad, nor sick, nor merry, nor well; but civil Count, civil as an orange. . . . (II. i. 290-1)

'Civil' indeed. Not *cold* to the extent of deserving our censure (Don John is the measure of coldness in this play), but *cool*. And altogether conventional.

While this 'civility' (in Beatrice's sense) is the ground or pervasive idiom of Claudio's personality, another and nicely associated trait soon becomes evident. Claudio lacks confidence in himself, and is readily given to suspecting others. The two features may seem distinct, but they spring in fact from a single root: a general uncertainty of outlook. Claudio is Don Pedro's constant shadow; each decision he takes must batten on his leader's authority. He cannot even trust the promptings of his own desires, but must seek confirmation of his feelings for Hero from both Benedick and Don Pedro (see I. i. 156ff.)—though he cannot have hoped for 'sober judgement' from the first. And despite his 'civil' regard for Don Petro, he accuses even him of insincerity when he offers advice:

> You speak this to fetch me in, my lord. (I. i. 214)

His subsequent readiness to believe that Don Pedro has cheated him and 'woos for himself' is just a rehearsal for his more dangerous readiness to suspect Hero's virtue when he hears it slandered. In both cases he is easy prey for Don John precisely because of a deeply-ingrained mistrust of his own feelings; he cannot exclude the possibility of his being quite wrong even about his most intimate beliefs. The contrast with Beatrice must strike us forcibly: she is utterly confident of her cousin's innocence —and Benedick, now at one with her through love, espouses her certainty. Again Claudio emerges as antitype of the other pair: his 'civil' nature adopts an exacerbated caution quite foreign to his friends' extrovert self-confidence.

The third trait, again linking nicely with those we know already, is more inferentially established, and partly by association of Claudio's personality with that of his chosen bride. It comes to the fore most notably at the moment of betrothal:

> *Claudio.* Silence is the perfectest herald of joy. I were but little happy if
> I could say how much. Lady, as you are mine, I am yours.
> I give away myself for you and dote upon the exchange.
> (II. i. 303-6)

Our first impulse, and rightly, is warm sympathy; in the theatre Claudio's hesitating acknowledgement with its language of reciprocal giving touches very movingly. Something, we feel, has been established. But our next reflection must be the fragility of the edifice. Hero is too embarrassed to reply, and Claudio, consonant with his self-mistrustful nature, manages very little speech himself. Both strike us as vulnerably young and inexperienced. It is a reflection strengthened both by Hero's preparation for marriage in III. iv. (she appears there as the young innocent apt to shy away from marriage's physical realities) and by Shakespeare's clearly deliberate keeping the pair apart until the Church scene—they have no opportunity to give evidence of wider knowledge and experience. The inference that we are meant to regard them both as vulnerable innocents (or rather their relationship as displaying vulnerable innocence) needs no further arguing.

When we assemble a personality out of these three traits, there will be no sense of incongruity if we see that personality as one readily inclined to adopt the procedures of the *mariage de convenance*. Evidently one who is by temperament conventional, lacking in self-confidence, and 'young' will find the modes of wooing laid down in arranged-marriage practice very much more tolerable than the intimate betrayals that come with Romance. To be able to rely on a senior friend, and to see the affair under the guise of unemotional arrangement, would clearly appeal. The Romance alternative he would find temperamentally very difficult to explore. With this said, we can, I think, reasonably claim that our theory is at least provisionally tenable, that it gives us a defensible way of looking at the play, and one that opens the way to a perception of why these two plots were brought together in a single comedy. More important, it allows the main plot to contribute to the study of 'love-in-courtship' with which all Shakespeare's mature comedies are concerned.

We still, however, have to ask what moral paradigm the Claudio plot presents, what, broadly, we discover (or 'learn') through imaginative sympathy with his experiences. We have laid stress on Claudio's early self-distrust and suspicion. These traits lead immediately to the first crisis he undergoes, his persuasion (as a result of Don John's hints) that Don Pedro 'woos for himself' and has stolen Hero's love. The incident is no more than an eddy in the broad stream of events, but it takes on significance through the striking language of Claudio's soliloquy:

> Friendship is constant in all other things
> Save in the office and affairs of love.
> Therefore all hearts in love use their own tongues;
> Let every eye negotiate for itself
> And trust no agent; for beauty is a witch
> Against whose charms faith melteth into blood.
> This is an accident of hourly proof,
> Which I mistrusted not. (II. i. 173-80)

The 'witch' metaphor evokes superbly the jealously-disposed lover's sense that beauty provides in itself a moral hazard (similar attitudes in *Hamlet* and *Othello* come to mind). More important for the moment is the associated reluctance to be trusting 'in the office and affairs of love'. Such an attitude is incompatible with being a lover; beyond all other relationships love necessitates the exercise of trust. And so, on the revelation that Don Pedro has, after all, performed his undertaking, the emphasis falls, in Claudio's betrothal-promise, on trust:

> Lady, as you are mine, I am yours. I give away myself for you and dote upon the exchange. (II. i. 304-6)

Self-giving expresses trust in its ultimate form; it places the whole of the lover's self at hazard, with no reservations and no safeguards. An attitude that stands in direct contrast to Claudio's earlier general suspicion.

The outline of the first complete sequence in Claudio's play-education is, then, just this: he moves from mistrust through a crisis to self-giving. It would obviously be a mistake to lay too much stress on these events, because, despite the potential of the love-acknowledgement as a touching moment in the theatre, we have with reason already commented on the superficiality and fragility of the liaison thus established. And yet this sequence, for all its lack of moral weight, does prefigure the larger design of Claudio's experience. In subjecting the Hero-Claudio relationship to the test of adversity (through the major intrigue of Don John's plot) *Much Ado* gives us the pattern of this first sequence writ large. As the 'education' of Beatrice and Benedick occurs in two stages (the garden-scenes and the 'Kill Claudio' episode), so does that of Claudio.

The initial aspect of this larger pattern needs little urging. Claudio's ready mistrust is patent; when Don John accuses Hero, as we have already seen, Claudio immediately suspects that the accusation is true. His self-giving commitment is rooted in too shallow a soil to withstand the villain's slander; 'conversion' from mistrust, like the parallel 'conversion' (of a different nature) of Beatrice and Benedick, can only become substantial under the pressure of the same distressful experience—the death (whether actual or as a reputation-metaphor) of Hero. The Friar indicates just how the crisis of Hero's supposed death will produce the desired effect:

> Marry, this well carried shall on her behalf
> Change slander to remorse; that is some good.
> But not for that dream I on this strange course,
> But on this travail look for greater birth. . . .
> When he shall hear she died upon his words,
> Th' idea of her life shall sweetly creep
> Into his study of imagination,
> And every lovely organ of her life
> Shall come appareled in more precious habit,
> More moving, delicate, and full of life,
> Into the eye and prospect of his soul
> Than when she lived indeed. (IV. i. 209-12; 222-9)

A momentous experience is obviously hinted at here; the 'remorse' that will follow the crisis of Hero's 'death' will only be the 'travail' to a 'greater birth', and this 'greater birth' will have the effect of transfiguring Hero until her image will be entertained by Claudio at the deepest levels of his being, in his 'soul'. Love will become a matter of total self-commitment, and not merely superficially so, as the betrothal-promise has proved.

*Much Ado* gives perhaps less direct emphasis to Claudio's 'conversion' than to Benedick's. To some extent we have to take it on trust, as part of the unconstrained new life of the play's ending. The new Claudio does however also appear in the dialogue. His response on hearing of Don John's treachery parallels, but is less profound than, the Friar's prophecy:

> Sweet Hero, now thy image doth appear
> In the rare semblance that I loved it first. (V. i. 252-3)

A redemption of his seeing has, he asserts, taken place, even if he makes no mention of Hero's image now being rooted in his 'soul'. And yet his new outlook represents a total reversal of the earlier self-absorbed figure:

> Choose your revenge yourself;
> Impose me to what penance your invention
> Can lay upon my sin. (V. i. 273-5)

A few lines later, after Leonato has suggested that he accept Hero's 'cousin' as his bride, the same attitude prevails:

> I do embrace your offer; and dispose
> For henceforth of poor Claudio. (V. i. 295-6)

The match with Hero's 'cousin' does indeed carry the bait of her position as heir to both Leonato and Antonio; but the stress should still fall on Claudio's willingness to accept her without any of the mistrustful probing which preceded, and then destroyed, his relationship with Hero. This is the aspect Shakespeare keeps before us. In the last scene Claudio approaches betrothal with a determination to 'hold my mind, were she an Ethiope'; he will ask no questions about her beauty or disposition. Remorse has at least conquered the earlier self-withholding tendencies in him. And when the masked Hero stands before him, he echoes the language of his previous betrothal:

> Give me your hand; before this holy friar
> I am your husband if you like of me. (V. iv. 58-59)

Now the language of self-giving has behind it the experience-validated realisation that mistrust easily credited can lead to disaster. In submitting to Leonato's request that he speak the betrothal promise before seeing his wife's face mistrust is symbolically rejected.

The stress on a newly-generous Claudio is, as we have said, light. For a modern audience it may tend to be lost in resistance to the 'unlikely' strategy of a masked Hero betrothed in such contrived circumstances to her 'other husband'. (Notice the implication of conversion in 'other'.) Even though we are not required to believe in a Hero actually dead and then revived, we tend to ask some more realistic outcome for love-narrative. But an Elizabethan, familiar with the conventions of Romance, would see in the apparently 'miraculous' re-birth of Hero a potent symbol for a new and ideal concord now fruitfully established; a concord within which her 'death' through mistrust could not again occur. We have already seen how the sense of life sailing out into the clear once more is given imaginative being verbally and theatrically. It is into this general context of optimistic expectation that the sense of a new orientation in Claudio's outlook is assumed; in a manner characteristic of comedy we believe in a new individuality for him, not so much because of overt signs in his behaviour, but because he now forms part of an altogether stable and generous environment.

It may be that Shakespeare miscalculated in his portrait of Claudio. Even when we understand the main features of his experience, we may still feel disinclined to give his marriage with Hero the total sympathy comedy asks. Because perhaps we find the particular individuality

Shakespeare thought to subject to 'the disciplinary experiences of love' too resistant to such experience, and because Claudio emerges at length, with our memory of his early ungenerous disposition still too potent for comfort. To put it another way, we may argue that the unlovable Claudio is too vividly and realistically portrayed (in the manner of a figure in tragedy) for us ever to credit a conversion to an appropriate marriage partner for Hero. F. P. Rossiter has suggested that in *Much Ado* Shakespeare's sensibility teetered on the brink of tragic perceptions, only retaining the comic equilibrium by a considerable effort of will (manifesting itself in the play-experience as a 'sense of withholding'). The figure of Claudio lends such an argument support; it harbours a potential for distressful experience too considerable to allow it to fit comfortably into the comic hypothesis.

We have so far traced the development of the leading personalities in both the main and secondary plots; we may now consider briefly the figure responsible for the crisis that provokes development. Not because he himself alters in a way that throws light on the play's meaning; rather because his unvarying nature highlights by contrast the positive values towards which Claudio, Beatrice and Benedick tend.

Don John's first appearance indicates at once his nature. He should almost certainly be costumed in black, the only sombre figure in the gaily-clad group. In total contrast to Leonato's overflowing hospitality and the voluble friendliness of all around him, he breaks silence grudgingly:

> I thank you. I am not of many words, but I thank you. (I. i. 152-3)

The egotism this suggests is more fully given in his later self-declaration:

> I had rather be a canker in a hedge than a rose in his grace, and it better fits my blood to be disdained of all than to fashion a carriage to rob love from any. In this, though I cannot be said to be a flattering honest man, it must not be denied but I am a plain-dealing villain. . . . If I had my mouth, I would bite; if I had my liberty, I would do my liking. In the meantime let me be that I am, and seek not to alter me. (I. iii. 25-35)

We notice here the insistent concern with self (I . . . I . . . I) and the hostile disposition towards others (it may be more than chance that he shares with the early Beatrice the key word 'disdain'). L. C. Knights, linking Don John with Richard of Gloucester (Richard III) and with Iago, observes that 'their common characteristic is an egotism that clenches itself hard against the claims of sympathy, and that is unwilling to change'.[1] Don John represents in an extreme form, in other words, the proud self-centredness away from which Beatrice and Benedick develop. Whereas their self-absorption expresses itself merely verbally, Don John's becomes active malice. His jealousy of Claudio (I. iii. 62-64), another characteristic he shares with Iago, leads him to seek the disruption of the marriage-process to which the whole play is dedicated. He and his henchmen Borachio and Conrade are therefore the only figures of appropriate social standing excluded from the marriage celebration with which the play ends; because the moral attitudes presupposed by marriage—the generous self-giving to which Beatrice, Benedick and Claudio come—cannot tolerate proud self-concern.

Don John's malice, it will be noted, is associated with sickness and poison (prefiguring in this too the methods of the tragic plays); appropriately, since an attitude inimical to the health of society is fitly imaged as inimical to the health of the body. In the passage quoted above 'canker' suggests a corrupting sickness as well as 'wild rose' (compare e.g. *Timon of Athens* IV. iii. 49); Don John's overthrow is 'a mortifying mischief' (I. iii. 12), to which he considers 'a moral medicine' inappropriate; Beatrice has only to look at him to be 'heartburned an hour after' (II. i. 4). Later the association becomes more explicit: Don John describes himself as 'sick in displeasure' to Claudio (II. ii. 5); he looks for the 'death of this marriage' (II. ii. 19) and Borachio assures him 'the poison of that lies in you to temper' (II. ii. 21). And of course the poison works, for Hero dies, in reputation if not in fact. Claudio's sensibility is also successfully contaminated: on coming to know through Borachio the evil he has done he exclaims: 'I have drunk poison whiles he uttered it' (V. i. 246). The image even appears in the garden-scene of the sub-plot; Hero explains:

> One doth not know
> How much an ill word may empoison liking. (III. i. 85-86)

—as it indeed poisons Claudio's liking for herself.

The moral design of *Much Ado* is completed therefore by a figure who

[1] L. C. Knights, 'The Question of Character in Shakespeare', in *More Talking of Shakespeare*, ed. John Garrett, 1959.

spells death to the positive goodness towards which the play works. Don John is of course the cardboard-thin villain of comedy; his presence cannot alter the comic orientation of the play because he is so simply and exclusively evil that we cannot think of him as a real personality, and so are not disturbed: we know throughout that his schemes must be defeated. His is barely in any sense a 'character in action', merely the catalyst that, as reminder of a non-idyllic, potentially destructive, world, brings about change in others.

# 4. The Intricate Texture

So far, we have talked of the overall emotional experience *Much Ado* yields, and said something of the play's moral discoveries. Out of these discussions a sense of the play's governing structure, of what it is 'about', has begun to emerge. We have seen how a three-step progression marks the play's emotional development: from gaiety through grave experience and on to a sense of confirmed and enduring happiness. We have further seen how, under the direct influence of such a context of events, the protagonists of the two plots achieve (at least token) moral development: Claudio, Beatrice and Benedick begin the play by being unfitted, in contrasting ways, for love; they end it in marriages we accept as exemplary. Yet these approaches, while they correspond to some part of our theatre-experience, leave us with a very strong sense that the unique quality of *Much Ado* still eludes us. In the theatre we experience a sense of the play's rich coherence, its possession of a distinguishing idiom; and we understand that it is precisely this possession that asks and wins our credence for the play's inherent comic assertion that 'all shall be well'. If we reflect further, we perhaps come to see that the play's idiom, its 'language' (in the widest sense), is a matter of intricate patterning. Where the tragic plays may rely largely on verbal means, the comedies often use as 'language' ideas or action-sequences that echo and mirror each other within a common idiom. So it is with *Much Ado*. Our task is now to discover and elaborate the presence of this common idiom within the play.

If we state at the outset, in a flat and provisional way, that the intrinsic 'language' of *Much Ado* springs from the near-omnipresence of mistakes and misconceptions of all kinds, we will have gone some way towards defining the play's idiom. But we would have to add that it is characteristic of these mistakes to lead, immediately or ultimately, to fortunate ends; whatever potential for catastrophe some of them enjoy, they will always, in the comically-devised world of *Much Ado*, promote happiness. Between these twin perceptions the comic integrity of *Much Ado* lies. The ways in which its discovered idiom relates to our already stated emotional and moral paradigms should become clear.

In ways obvious and less so, the Dogberry and Verges episodes share in this common idiom; indeed it might be argued that the Watch's very existence and the way in which they arrest the Don John intrigue figure in little the play's general comic perception. The amusement afforded by Dogberry and Verges and their fellows lies largely in their total incomprehension of the task to which they are assigned. For citizens deputed to act as the Prince's Watch they are sublimely ignorant of the nature of their duties; Dogberry's charge (III. iii. 9ff.) succeeds in defining precisely how a Watch should *not* behave if it is to perform efficiently its task of putting down disorder in the commonwealth. Perfect peace will be achieved for the Watch themselves, but only at the cost of allowing crime and disturbance of all kinds to thrive. One Watchman puts the matter succinctly:

We will rather sleep than talk; we know what belongs to a watch. (III. iii. 38-39)

(An Elizabethan sense of 'to watch' was 'to keep awake'). And, while they do certainly take Conrade and Borachio into custody, the charges they prefer against them involve misunderstandings of every sort, including a firm conviction that 'one Deformed' has been an accessory to this 'most dangerous piece of lechery'. Dogberry's conduct of the trial and his report on the incident to Leonato ensure that confusion is worse confounded; whenever Verges approaches the point of speaking sense Dogberry apologises for his neighbour's incompetence, and prevents discovery. And yet, despite blunderings of every conceivable description, Don John's malicious scheme is thwarted. As the comic world is structured, good will always triumph; and in *Much Ado* not through the vigilance of the wise (Claudio's suspicious observation is deceived), but through chance and the mistakings of the incompetent. Borachio makes the point explicitly:

What your wisdoms could not discover, these shallow fools have brought to light. (V. i. 231-3)

The way in which the play's major crisis is resolved corresponds therefore to the perception roughly outlined above: in the *Much Ado* world mistakings lead eventually to fortunate results.

The Dogberry and Verges episodes are knit into the play's idiom even more closely than this. Not only do the two neighbours act as the

D

Prince's Watch and by their behaviour parody the strained vigilance of, particularly, Claudio, they are also assigned, improbably enough, to the task of conducting a trial. In a play (itself a species of trial) the establishment of a court of law may act as an opportunity for achieving true judgement: as it does in *The Merchant of Venice* and (though not so formally) in the last scene of *Measure for Measure*. (Later examples in *King Lear* and *The Winter's Tale*, very different as they are, reward comparative study; *The Tempest* may, as a whole, be considered an extended trial.) In *Much Ado* also, true judgement does emerge; the Sexton is enabled (IV. ii. 6off.) to gather from the proceedings the truth about Don John's villany. But the actual conduct of the case parodies in detail the accepted procedures of law. Again we must visualise the scene; the lay-out of the stage and the position of the various characters would recall the appearance of a law-court in session; Dogberry, Verges and the Sexton would enter with as fair an imitation as they could of the dignity of the justiciary, and all three would be gowned. The incongruity between the concepts invoked (the majesty of law) and the individuals concerned will have been at once apparent. Dogberry much enhances this visual perception by his behaviour. After gravely denying the very existence of the Court ('our whole dissembly') he goes on to confuse the distinction between judge and criminal by claiming for himself and Verges the title of 'malefactors'. (The same point is made with the utmost seriousness, at *Lear* IV. i. 161ff.: the links between comedy and tragedy might usefully be pondered from such a parallel as this.) Dogberry then proceeds to bungle the examination and misinterpret the evidence before him; he also burlesques the impartiality of law, and inverts the most sacred premise of British justice: that a man is innocent till proved guilty. At the outset of the trial he exclaims:

> Masters it is proved already that you are little better than false knaves, and it will go near to be thought so shortly. (IV. ii. 20-22)

The sentence he imposes is appropriate to a trial that begins by misconceiving the law so drastically;

> O villain! Thou wilt be condemned into everlasting redemption for this. (IV. ii. 55-56)

The scene's closing insistence on Dogberry's being 'writ down an ass' stems from the worthy constable's desire to have recorded an outrage

on his dignity and position; the audience rightly takes it as a true statement of fact. And yet out of all this absurd inversion of good sense and
true justice there emerges a fortunate state of affairs: Hero's reputation
is saved and Claudio 'converted'. Such is the idiom of this play. The
baffling of true judgement leads, immediately or ultimately, to happiness.

We have so far said little of Dogberry's most widely-known characteristic, his apparently infinite capacity for distorting the meaning of
words. Illustration is unnecessary; almost every speech affords examples.
In this too he is linked with another aspect of the main and sub-plots.
His absurd adventures among words make him a sort of inverting mirror
of the wit of Beatrice and Benedick. Where these two *wilfully* mis-
manage words, Dogberry does so in total innocence; where they are
masters of language, he is its thrall. And he mistakes words with something of the same fertility of invention as they; the zestful exuberance of
Benedick/Beatrice flytings finds its counterpart in the abundant energy
Dogberry brings to addressing the Watch or Leonato (the magnificent
'tediousness' of III. v.) or Conrade and Borachio. It might even be
argued that his pride in his achievements (both of position and of language) render him a fitting parallel to the proud Beatrice and Benedick
of the early acts. As the play shows, the basis of the wits' pride is as
mistaken as the basis of Dogberry's own.

In ways such as these we see how the intricate design of *Much Ado*
provides for the mirroring in the Dogberry/Verges episodes of themes
and attitudes from the two major plots. The theme of mistaking, so
prevalent (as we shall see) in both, finds here its broadest statement: the
Watch's total incapacity and incomprehension, Dogberry's blunderings
among words and the absurdities of the trial are a caricature-develop-
ment of various types of blindness, of mistaking, in the rest of the play.
It is significant that Shakespeare should employ such broad fools as these
to unravel in ignorance *Much Ado*'s most serious complication: the
comic perception that 'all shall be well' is strongly emphasised by being
made dependent upon the good offices of such clowns.

The analysis of themes tends to make a play seem a very abstract
thing; we have almost drained away the robust comic humour of the
Dogberry and Verges episodes by talking about them in this way. In the
theatre we should be conscious mainly of the near farce of the Watch's
appearance and drill, and of the absurd interplay between the two
neighbours. It might therefore be thought that discussion of themes is

a mere academic impertinence. But what we painstakingly analyse here is what determines in the theatre the precise nature of our unconscious experience—the experience we can only describe afterwards by saying that the play 'hung together' or was 'persuasive' or 'had consistency'. Analysis can show how this 'consistency', this persuasion of significance is developed; in the theatre we respond to it imaginatively without further prompting—though the more experienced we are in drama the more readily and fully we will respond. As we dissect the play to show its singularly intricate patterning (or some of it) we can come to understand the comic perception, abstractly expressed, to which production gives imaginative life.

Writing of the meaning of *Much Ado*, F. P. Rossiter discovers throughout the play what he calls 'a complex harmony of interdependent themes'. These themes, he claims, are expressed through 'misapprehensions, misprisions, misunderstandings, misinterpretations and misapplications.' The essential mode of the play, in other words, is said to be the functioning of illusion; and the outcome of illusion (Rossiter could have added) is always fortunate. Having seen this idiom at work in the Dogberry and Verges episodes, we may now attempt to locate at least some of the manifestations of illusion in the two major plots. We shall then ask how these interact and combine to form the 'world', both verbal and visual, of *Much Ado*, and say something of why Shakespeare should have chosen this particular idiom for a play about 'love in courtship'.

The most convenient way of beginning is to trace the narrative thread (the paradigm of event) in both plots, and see how it involves the functioning of illusion. Again it is simplest to begin with Beatrice and Benedick. These two open the play by 'acting the part' of love's antagonists; the self-centredness of their wit is much more a matter of conscious rôle-playing than of natural inclination. Benedick goes so far as to acknowledge that being 'a professed tyrant to their sex' is a matter of 'custom' (I. i. 162-3); Claudio uses the language of acting to claim, substantially unchallenged, that this 'obstinate heretic in the despite of beauty' 'never could *maintain his part* but in the force of his will' (I. i. 225-8). The same is true of Beatrice; she conducts her 'merry war' as a matter of adopting a persona rather than as a matter of conviction; Leonato implies as much at I. i. 58-61. Their initial attitude is, in other words, a matter of illusion in the sense that an actor's part is illusion; their real instincts are masked by an assumed persona. And not only is their first position a matter of playing a part; the means by which they are 'converted' from it directly involves acting, pretence, under a guise only superficially different. In the garden scenes Claudio, Don Pedro and Leonato, Hero and Ursula, *play the part* of sympathetic friends allegedly discussing quite imaginary disclosures by, in one case, Beatrice, in the other Benedick. These scenes are in fact virtually little plays-within-the-play, with the conspirators as actors and Beatrice and Benedick for audience. Shakespeare preserves the verisimilitude of acting even to the extent of allowing Leonato to 'dry' and having Claudio and Don Pedro cover his lapse (II. iii. 113-16). Both scenes are prepared in language that recalls the theatre; and both make internal use of words like 'counterfeit': complicating the issue so finely as to allow the momentary suggestion by Don Pedro that perhaps Beatrice merely 'counterfeits' passion—a passion that exists only in their own collective imagination (II. iii. 105). The idiom of illusion could hardly go further. The immediate outcome for Benedick is that he misinterprets into love-language Beatrice's perfectly innocent announcement of dinner; later each stalks the other under the mistaken belief (entertained until the play's last scene) that he or she has confessed to despairing love. So the dynamic of illusion persists. Benedick's love is tested, as we have seen, within the context of grave emotions associated with the *pretended* death of Hero; and that pretended death issues, as the audience is aware, from Don John's wholly false allegations. Each step in the Beatrice–Benedick plot, in other words, is attended by illusion; until with the metaphor-strengthened dawning of a new day the final scene at length sets illusions aside, and marriage is celebrated.

As the idiom of the secondary plot is that of illusion, so also is it of the main plot. Claudio's experience is at once a parallel and a contrast: parallel in the sense that his ultimate marriage with Hero emerges once again out of mistakings—pretence—contrasted in the sense that mistakings act in his case as threats to already existing love rather than as factors making towards a love relationship. To an extent, the Claudio plot could be said to present the functioning of illusion at a later stage in a love-relationship; where it becomes in fact, within the context of existing love, potential for jealousy and rejection. And yet here too, as in the secondary plot, illusion works towards a positive end, the establishment in Claudio and Hero of a true and experience-vindicated love: such is the structuring of the comic world. To be more specific: Claudio's first deception arises, like Benedick's, out of circumstances that involve pretence, even a species of overhearing. Claudio behind his mask (II. i. 159ff.) disclaims his own identity, preferring to 'act the part' of Benedick; he then 'overhears', as it were, Don John's insinuation that his brother 'woos for himself'; the result is his dejected belief, based on false premises, that he is rivalled in love by one he had trusted. The whole sequence of events is determined by illusion; the outcome, consistent with comic expectations, is fortunate: reassurance and the betrothal with Hero. The major deception of the play, Don John's, involves a type of illusion by now familiar. Although it takes place off stage, we know from various anticipatory and subsequent descriptions (II. ii. 41ff.; IV. i. 88ff.; V. i. 236ff.) that it required a play-sequence, with Margaret playing the part of Hero and Borachio that of an unnamed lover; Claudio and Don Pedro overhear their amorous talk and mistakenly infer Hero's unchastity. The final main-plot sequence is again steeped in illusion; after the pretence of Hero's death, and Claudio's resultant homage at her tomb, he accepts her hand under circumstances that necessitate her playing the part of an imaginary 'cousin'; it is only after Claudio has submitted to this illusion that he finds himself marrying 'Hero that was dead'. So illusion, omnipresent in this as in the secondary plot, has again a fortunate outcome, confirmed by marriage.

The paradigm of event in both plots shows how essential to their functioning illusion is. Yet it is written into the play even more intimately than this. The little scene I. ii. may be described as largely impertinent to either plot; Antonio's belief that Don Pedro is in love with Hero, engendered by a servant's mistaken overhearing (a deliberate prefiguring of the garden scenes: notice its setting), has no issue whatever in action. All it does—a matter of at least equal significance—is to aggravate the climate of illusion within which the play works. The idiom of overhearing is carried on in the next scene. Don John, who might have gathered the news through any channel, in fact hears of Claudio's love for Hero as the result of a servant's eavesdropping. (I. iii. 56ff.). This particular report is true; but it is characteristic of the Messina world in that it came not directly, but from concealment: just as Claudio learns the (false) news of Don Pedro's rivalry from the concealment of a mask, and later the false news of Hero's unchastity from some hiding-place; just as the Watch overhear Borachio discussing Don John's treachery under the shelter of night; and just as Benedick hears the (false-yet-true) report of Beatrice's love from the concealment of an 'arbor'. So this incident partakes too of the indirections of the play-world; and illusion (or potential-for-illusion) proliferates. Even to the extent of making the subject of Balthazar's song the contention that 'men were *deceivers* ever'; and of making us uncertain about the quality of his performance (on this matter of subjective, and hence on one view illusory, judgement, Don Pedro, Benedick and Balthazar himself disagree). The little dialogue at the opening of II. iii. between Benedick and the boy (who never reappears with the book asked for) may be described as almost inane; but it may also rehearse once more the dominant theme: even the most ordinary sentences are open to mis-interpretation; like, it seems, all communication in the Messina world.

The most suggestive visual symbol for all this is the masked dance (II. i. 85ff.). Each of the characters interposes between himself and his partner the 'false face' of a mask. They thus typify the concealments integral to the *Much Ado* idiom. Antonio goes so far as to deny his true identity when the disguise is pierced, Benedick refuses to reveal his, and Claudio a few lines later claims to be Benedick. By this means is pre-sented, visually as well as verbally, the play-acting tendencies of the Messina world, where a character may at any moment assume a mask or persona distinct from his own identity. And where indeed personae are attributed to individuals without their knowledge: Claudio here claims to be Benedick; during the twin garden scenes Beatrice and Benedick are in turn described, without foundation, as the love-lorn personae they later, to a large extent, become; Hero, as a result of Don John's arranged 'play', has thrust upon her the persona of a wanton. The incidents of the masked dance are perhaps even more carefully designed than this. On each side of Antonio's desperate insistence upon playing any part but his own are dialogues which refer to the play's twin themes, falling in love and slander. The first two record courtship (and the checks to courtship) and the last (Beatrice/Benedick) records slander (in a comic vein): all are conducted within the context of deceiving masks. Thus the illusions of the play are focused in miniature. The play's comic thesis emerges visually when this dance is recalled by the dance with which *Much Ado* ends: there all masks are laid aside (the ladies wear them in the early part of the scene) and we take in the significance that now illusions are banished, purposes clear and identities known. The pattern of the dance becomes a celebration of personal and social order, as all the couples submit to its controlling rhythms; the earlier, masked, dance was akin rather to treading the mazes of illusion. A valid production might well make the point by offering contrasted styles of dance.

This pervasive interest in illusion is carried at the level of dialogue largely by references to seeing, and seeing falsely (the counterpart of overhearing and misreporting in action). A selection of some of the more notable occurrences will indicate how the development of both plots may be traced in terms of metaphors of sight. Claudio early asserts that 'in mine eye [Hero] is the sweetest lady that ever I looked on' (I. i. 181); when he thinks her base he exclaims repeatedly against the 'seeming' in her which makes false his eyes' report (IV. i. 32ff.); in order to sub-stantiate his deceitful practice Don John challenges Claudio: 'If you dare not trust that you see, confess not that you know' (III. ii. 115-16) and Borachio ultimately admits 'I have deceived even your very eyes' (V. i. 231). Claudio's recovery of illusion-free judgement is given, again, in terms of seeing; the Friar predicts that Hero's true image will establish itself in 'the eye and prospect of his soul' (IV. i. 228) and Claudio himself later confirms that a redemption of his sight has in fact taken place (V. i. 252-3). In the Beatrice-Benedick plot the sight of the eye is again the prominent metaphor. Both characters begin by claiming 'good sight', the counterpart of their wit-defended pride. To Claudio's infatuated praise of Hero Benedick replies, 'I can see yet without spectacles, and I see no such matter' (I. i. 183-4); Beatrice claims, 'I have a good eye, uncle; I can see a church [sc. where marriage is solemnised] by daylight' (II. i. 81-2). And yet Beatrice's eyes, where 'disdain and scorn ride sparkling', are made subject to the illusions of love; Margaret reflects 'how you may be converted I know not; but methinks you look with your eyes as other women do' (III. iv. 88-89). Those eyes have in fact already adopted the 'new seeing' of love, as Benedick's had almost immediately after his closely similar enquiry: 'May I be so converted and see with these eyes?' (II. iii. 22-23). The clarifications of the last scene include a statement of the twin capitulation:

*Benedick.*   Signior Leonato, truth it is, good signior,
              Your niece regards me with an eye of favor.
*Leonato.*    That eye my daughter lent her; 'tis most true.

*Benedick.*    And I do with an eye of love requite her.
*Leonato.*    The sight whereof I think you had from me,
        From Claudio, and the Prince. (V. iv. 21-26).

Both plots depend therefore, at the level of dialogue, on the education of the eye: in one case *out of* the misapprehensions of suspicion (and into a more inward unsuspicious seeing), in the other *into* the 'new seeing' of love. The appropriateness of metaphors from sight to a play which moves through illusion to clarification need not be insisted upon.

The above paragraphs merely summarise the functioning of illusion in *Much Ado*, and indicate some of its various forms; the reader will discover other occurrences for himself. An important question remains however to ask: why did Shakespeare select this idiom for a play that traces the fortunes of love-in-courtship? What does *Much Ado* 'tell' us about the nature of that particular experience?

A full answer would involve quite simply a reprint, or rather per-formance, of the play. *Much Ado is* the statement we are looking for. But we may be able to approach a performance (or at any rate the interpretation of a performance) with more confidence, if we understand how the theme of illusion is appropriate to the experience of falling in love, and to its opposite, the rejection of love. The former case can be greatly clarified by looking at another of Shakespeare's comedies, *A Midsummer Night's Dream*. There the mistakings incident to falling in love are explicitly presented: in the confusions of the action in the wood, initiated by Puck's love-juice, and also in, notably, Titania's love for the monstrous Bottom. The originating perception of the play might be traced back to some words spoken by Helena at I. i. 232-6, words that serve as commentary on the sight metaphor we found dominant in both plots of *Much Ado* (it will be found at least equally widespread in *A Midsummer Night's Dream*; Puck anoints the lovers' *eyes*):

> Things base and vile, holding no quantity,
> Love can transpose to form and dignity.
> Love looks not with the eyes, but with the mind,
> And therefore is winged Cupid painted blind.
> Nor hath Love's mind of any judgement taste;
> Wings, and no eyes, figure unheedy haste.

The crucial lines are the third and fifth. Once we dissociate 'mind' from the specifically intellectual and rational processes, and understand that it refers to personal, affective, emotional responses, the significance of the lines will become clear. Helena is contrasting love with *objective* responses ('judgement' and unanointed eyes); the love-response is individual, subjective, and hence may be idiosyncratic. The lover's 'mind', in other words, dictates what he sees, not a more objective assessment. The delusions and fantasies to which 'blind Cupid' subjects his victims verge, from one point of view, on madness; but when stabilised and confirmed by 'Dian's bud' they also 'grow to something of great constancy' (see the Theseus-Hippolyta dialogue opening Act V). The main point for us is that the lover's eye, by virtue of the very fact of being a *lover's*, is peculiarly liable to delusion; delusion is indeed the very idiom of its experience. In *Much Ado*, this perception is broadened to include not only eyes, but ears also (the overhearing theme); and extends even further, to indicate that not only does the experience itself consist of delusory elements, but may indeed spring from misinterpretations of fact. David L. Stevenson is right to insist, in his introduction to the Signet edition, on the play's 'sustained, mimetic realism', for *Much Ado* is concerned with the context, as well as the experience of love; both may be imbued with illusion.[1] It is therefore appropriate that a narrative dealing with the establishment of love should be set, as it is in *Much Ado*, within the context of all-pervasive illusion. Both the nature of the experience, and the circumstances of its occurrence, are thus communicated.

The relevance of illusion to *being* in love, and lapsing from it, is perhaps more immediately evident. Love is the most vulnerable of relationships precisely because its continued existence may depend upon the lover being satisfied that his love is returned; hence if the personal judgement (the only index of this) is deluded, love may be destroyed. This is at least true of love that is less than totally self-committing, less than the love that asks and expects no return. Claudio's love, in a quite natural and credible way, does ask return; and so it collapses when his personal judgement is deluded as to the state of Hero's affections. Illusion may have, in this way, a perfectly familiar, destructive, effect. And there, in tragedy, the play would end. But the thesis of comedy that 'all

---

[1] There is no conflict between the discovered 'realism' and 'illusion'; the existence of illusion is presented within a world 'created in very close imitation of the habitable one we know outside the theatre' (Stevenson, p. xxii). The *Much Ado* world is at least 'very real' compared with that of, say, *As You Like It* or *A Midsummer Night's Dream*.

shall be well' attributes to delusion a further, therapeutic, potential: under the delusion that Hero is dead Claudio's love is rendered fit for his marriage to 'another Hero'. Remorse is not, in the comically-structured world, a helpless, laggard emotion; circumstances are so ordered as to allow it fruitful effect, not only for the grieving individual, but also as rescinding the evil deed itself.

It should be clear, therefore, how the functioning of illusion permeates *Much Ado* with entire appropriateness; its incidence to falling in love, love's rejection and love's maturing, vindicate its use as the play's peculiar language. If we wished, now, to put together a very rough paraphrase of the *Much Ado* experience (while recognising the dangers of such an activity) we might argue that the play allows us imaginative entry into a world where illusion enjoys *comic* potential, where illusion makes, in other words, for the success (in all its aspects) of love-in-courtship.

# 5. The Continuing Concern

*Much Ado* is governed, we have more than once observed, by the comic hypothesis that 'all shall be well'; the play-experience exercises and satisfies the instinct within us for interpreting life as benignly structured. And yet the factor which most markedly distinguishes *Much Ado* from other comedies of its date is the sense that this hypothesis is under strain, that the outlook conveyed is somehow precarious, maintained wilfully rather than with an easy naturalness. We may properly speak of *Much Ado* as the 'gayest' of Shakespeare's comedies; it is certainly (to use Dover Wilson's terminology) not the 'happiest'. That this is not wayward fancy, but stems from sensitive reading of the text, can be demonstrated. The passages of dramatic poetry which strike us as displaying a peculiar forcefulness, suggestive of intensely personal origins, are often passages that reflect on distressful or potentially distressful experience: Claudio's 'beauty is a witch' speech, his tirades against 'seeming' in the Church scene, or Leonato's grief-stricken lines in Act V. The distress that finds embodiment in these speeches, and others, is held in check by the play's governing hypothesis; yet the pressure it exerts cannot be entirely denied. With very little shift in our angle of vision we can readily believe in a world which lacks Dogberry and Verges to avert, in ignorance, the plot's inclination towards disaster; a world where circumstances *assist* Don John, and Hero dies in reality, not only in metaphor. There is no question of this being a world truer or less true than the world of comic vision; it is simply different, and complementary.

That world comes to exist, of course, as the determining hypothesis of many of Shakespeare's later plays; the pressures held in check in *Much Ado* there enjoy free play as the agents of a tragic vision. Where illusion in comedy makes for confirmed happiness and order, in the tragically-inclined plays it leads to disruption and catastrophe. Claudio's exclamations against 'seeming'—eventually productive of good in his world—become in later plays Troilus' distressed perception that 'this is and is not Cressid', or Hamlet's unbalancing recognition of the gap that opens between what is and what appears (his poignant initial self-declaration runs: 'I know not seems'). Later again, the occlusions of vision in Lear and Gloucester, leading them to confuse true and false affection, lead to a disastrous outcome. More striking than these for the student of *Much Ado* is the manner in which illusion wreaks havoc in *Othello*, a tragedy that shares many structural similarities with the main plot of the earlier play. To compare and contrast Claudio's part with Othello's, Hero's with Desdemona's, and Don John's with Iago's, and to discover when doing so the functioning of illusion in the tragedy, would be to throw useful light on both plays, and lead to a fuller knowledge of Shakespeare's philosophy of love, its precarious dependence on personal vision and its vulnerability to suspicious vigilance. Such an exercise may also suggest the senses in which Shakespeare's total output is a unity, certain common themes being reconsidered at different points in his career, and the insights gained never completely jettisoned in favour of new material and new interests.

It would lie quite beyond the scope of this essay to relate *Much Ado* in a more detailed way to Shakespeare's later work. One further glance ahead will have to stand as a way of suggesting how this comedy, while a complete theatrical experience in itself, is also markedly seminal for future plays. Near the end of his career as dramatist, Shakespeare was again able to bring illusion-in-love within the hypothesis of comedy. Leontes' self-engendered jealousy and its effects (in *The Winter's Tale*) are more concentratedly appalling even than Othello's; the jealousy is based on a suspicious vigilance that recalls both Othello's and Claudio's; it produces disruption on a personal, social and even political level. The method of resolving its effects, at any rate for Leontes himself, recalls very distinctly the final scene in *Much Ado*. When Leontes 'wakes his faith', and the 'statue' of Hermione comes, in response, to life, we may hear distant echoes of the way in which Claudio, matured to become a fit marriage-partner for Hero, finds her 'come back to life'. Again there are, of course, very wide differences between the two plays; Shakespeare could not have written Leontes' part before undergoing imaginatively the profoundly disturbing experience of the tragedies; the resolution consequently calls into play levels of awareness untapped in *Much Ado*. And yet, the formal similarities indicate that the earlier play symbolises at its own level a conviction to which Shakespeare was to return, with much developed powers and insight, at the end of his dramatic career. If we have begun to understand *Much Ado* in other words, we have begun to understand a perception close to the centre of Shakespeare's dramatic imagination.

# Some Further Reading

H. B. Charlton, *Shakespeare's Comedies* (1938)

J. R. Brown, *Shakespeare and His Comedies*, (second ed., 1962)

D. L. Stevenson, *The Love-Game Comedy* (1946)

F. P. Rossiter, Chapter on *Much Ado* in '*Angel with Horns*' *and other Shakespeare Lectures*, ed. Graham Storey (1961)

Graham Storey, 'The Success of *Much Ado About Nothing*', in *More Talking of Shakespeare*, ed. John Garrett (1959)

J. C. Maxwell, 'Shakespeare's Middle Plays', *The Age of Shakespeare*, *Pelican Guide to English Literature*, II (1955)

F. Kermode, 'The Mature Comedies', in *The Early Shakespeare*, ed. Bernard Harris and J. R. Brown (1961)

# Index